The Sage of Time and Chance

The Sage of Time and Chance

Kathleen L. Housley

RESOURCE *Publications* · Eugene, Oregon

THE SAGE OF TIME AND CHANCE

Copyright © 2015 Kathleen L. Housley. All rights reserved. Except for brief quotations in critical publications or reviews, no part of this book may be reproduced in any manner without prior written permission from the publisher. Write: Permissions. Wipf and Stock Publishers, 199 W. 8th Ave., Suite 3, Eugene, OR 97401.

Resource Publications
An Imprint of Wipf and Stock Publishers
199 W. 8th Ave., Suite 3
Eugene, OR 97401

www.wipfandstock.com

ISBN 13: 978-1-4982-0178-0

Manufactured in the U.S.A.   01/09/2015

In memory of Richard DeBold who read an early draft of *The Sage of Time and Chance*, saw its potential, and argued vehemently with me about the nature of chance. Not long before he died, he wrote on the first page, "Remember everything is accidental but lawful. We just don't yet know the laws."

Introduction

The Sage of Time and Chance is a work of fiction based on Ecclesiastes, the most skeptical book in the Bible. Ecclesiastes was written by a person who had the audacity to question whether humans were any different from animals. Confounded by the limits of the human mind, the writer was convinced that the righteous and the wise were not rewarded by God, nor were the unrighteous and the foolish punished. Time and chance happened to them all.

The name Ecclesiastes is rooted in Greek meaning a member of the assembly. Sometimes it has been taken to mean either teacher or preacher. The name in Hebrew is Qoheleth, transliterated as Koheleth, alluding to someone who gathers together, be it a gathering of people, proverbs, or possessions. The name also alludes to a convocation.

In the ancient world, it was common practice for the authorship of wisdom literature to be attributed to rulers while the real authors remained anonymous. It is no surprise that the first verse of Ecclesiastes states, "The words of the teacher, the son of David, king in Jerusalem," the assumption being that it is written by King Solomon who ruled in the tenth century BCE. However, the actual author implies at various places in the book that he is a sage or official who has served in the royal court, even offering readers advice on proper behavior when in the presence of the king. The use of some Persian words in the book also puts its authorship much later than the time of Solomon, in fact, after the Babylonian exile. For these reasons, I have set the story in Jerusalem during the time of Ptolemy II Philadelphus who ruled over Ptolemaic Egypt, including Israel, from 283 to 246 BCE, a relatively peaceful period rich in scholarship and culture. Not only did

Introduction

Ptolemy expand the magnificent Library at Alexandria, he also exchanged ambassadors with lands as far away as India.

Ecclesiastes was included in the Septuagint, the translation of the Hebrew Scriptures into Greek done in Alexandria during the Ptolemaic period. The book called *Ecclesiasticus*, also known as *The Wisdom of Joshua Ben Sira*, was written in Jerusalem and translated by Joshua's grandson in Alexandria. Despite the similarity of names and their both being in the category of wisdom literature, there is no known link between Ecclesiastes and Ecclesiasticus, which was written during the reign of Ptolemy III Euergetes.

In *The Sage of Time and Chance*, Koheleth convenes an assembly at the end of the celebration of Sukkot, the joyful pilgrim festival that takes place each fall in remembrance of the exodus from Egypt and the forty years of wandering in the desert. Beginning with the Biblical command in Leviticus 23:42, the central event during Sukkot is the construction of temporary booths out of leafy boughs in which families live for a week. However, prior to the destruction of the temple in Jerusalem in 70 CE, Sukkot combined aspects of a harvest festival with dramatic temple rituals linked to the coming of rain. There is a wealth of fact, tradition, and folklore surrounding Sukkot. One set of stories is about heavenly guests, usually patriarchs, who visit the booth at night one at a time. In *The Sage of Time and Chance*, the guests are translators and writers, including Jerome who translated Ecclesiastes into Latin, and Saadia ben Yosef who translated it into Arabic.

The Greek historian Herodotus (fifth century BCE) helped shape the international perspective of the Grecian world. He also stressed the value of collecting and remembering facts and stories. I used his stories about gold-guarding griffins, fierce Amazons, and warlike Scythians to increase the scope of *The Sage of Time and Chance*. Doing so was important, because there were powerful Jewish communities in foreign countries, including Egypt and Persia. Because of the diaspora, the Jewish world was not as small as Biblical scholars sometimes make it appear.

Alexander the Great is another historical figure who plays an important background role in *The Sage of Time and Chance*. At the time of his death in 323 BCE at the age of 32, Alexander had cast a very long shadow over the world, spreading Hellenism all the way to India. Using battering rams and siege-towers, he brutally destroyed the city of Tyre in 332 BCE. Then he marched his highly trained army south, bypassing Jerusalem but annihilating Gaza. Because Jerusalem was spared, Jewish stories generally present him in a more benign light than he deserves. Although there is no

Introduction

mention of Alexander in Ecclesiastes, one of the book's themes is oppression. Writing that "power is on the side of the oppressors," Ecclesiastes concludes it is better for the oppressed to be dead or to have never been born.

Twentieth century theologians to whom I am indebted for broadening my perspective include Martin Buber, Abraham Heschel, and Dietrich Bonhoeffer, specifically Buber's *Tales of the Hasidim: Early Masters*, Heschel's *Who Is Man?*, and Bonhoeffer's *Letters and Papers from Prison*. In a statement with which Ecclesiastes would have concurred, Buber described his standpoint as not resting "on the broad upland of a system that includes a series of sure statements about the absolute, but on a narrow ridge between gulfs where there is no sureness of expressible knowledge but the certainty of meeting what remains undisclosed." Heschel grappled with the question who is man, writing that man is "a being in travail with God's dreams and designs, with God's dream of a world redeemed, of reconciliations of heaven and earth, of a mankind which is truly His image, reflecting His wisdom, justice and compassion."

Bonhoeffer shared with Ecclesiastes a great concern about the nature of folly, a topic with which he dealt brilliantly in his essay *After Ten Years*. As Bonhoeffer's situation in a Nazi prison grew more and more dire leading up to his execution by hanging on April 9, 1945, Ecclesiastes was one of the books to which he turned, finding solace in the passage about God "seeking again that which has passed away." However, in his book *Ethics*, drafted before his imprisonment, Bonhoeffer embraced the joyful passages as well, including Ecclesiastes 9:7, "Go eat your bread with gladness and drink your wine with a joyful heart."

Additional background notes and scriptural references are included at the end of *The Sage of Time and Chance*. For my own benefit, I translated Ecclesiastes from Hebrew, using the *Biblia Hebraica Stuttgartensia*. However, my skills in Hebrew are not high enough to translate adequately the many linguistic ambiguities in Ecclesiastes that stem in part from the use of loanwords in Persian and Aramaic. To increase my understanding, I turned to *Ecclesiastes* by Choon-Leong Seow in the Anchor Bible series. An internationally recognized Hebrew scholar, Seow's knowledge of Ecclesiastes is encyclopedic. I also consulted several English translations: the New Revised Standard Version, the International Version, the New English Bible, and, for sheer beauty of language, the King James Version. Also important was *Ecclesiastes Through the Centuries* by Eric S. Christianson, part of the

INTRODUCTION

Blackwell Bible Commentaries, which is a fascinating study of the influence of Ecclesiastes on culture, art, and literature.

But ultimately—and thankfully—Ecclesiastes slips through the confining nets of all translations, including mine. As it is written, "All streams flow to the sea but the sea is never full."

Kathleen L. Housley

1

All Streams Flow to the Sea

"Mist mist all is *mist.*" Koheleth murmurs the words so softly no one else in the great hall hears. While he listens for the congruence of sound and meaning, he senses inwardly that his silver life thread is stretched taut, and his golden bowl has developed fine cracks that are spreading steadily from the base to the rim. He wonders if he has enough time to do what must be done before the thread snaps and the bowl shatters. For a moment only, Koheleth pulls on his gray beard and gazes up at the high ceiling with its sturdy cedar beams imported from the distant mountains of Lebanon. Then he gives his head a slight shake and forces his mind back to the problem at hand, which is how to phrase the opening line of his untitled scroll.

"*Emptiness, emptiness all is emptiness.*" If he uses that word instead of *mist*, will the reader be able to differentiate between the subtle gradations of meanings: either a permanent void or a space with the potent capability of being filled? Is the hollow stem of a reed flute empty? What of a water pitcher broken at the well? Is the earth empty of sound just because Koheleth's ears have lost the capacity to hear distinctly? Is it bleached of color because he cannot see clearly? Such foolish rhetorical questions! Yes, it has been a long time since Koheleth last heard the soft cooing of the doves at sunrise; nonetheless, he does not doubt they continue to coo for his children and grandchildren. He has difficulty reading (throughout his life a source of contentment, even astonishment), his eyes becoming so tired that the letters blur after only a few paragraphs. But that problem is pleasantly ameliorated by having someone read aloud to him. So also, only if his friends and family come near can he discern their distinctive features—the slight crook in his son's nose from the time he fell out of the fig tree, the jagged scar on his daughter's right cheek where she was scratched by a pet panther, up until then considered quite tame. He does not need to see those marks to be certain they remain.

"*Vanity of vanities, vanity of vanities, all is vanity. What does a man gain from all his labor, toiling under the sun? Generations go and generations come, but the earth stays forever. The sun also rises and the sun sets and hurries to its place where it arose.*" Koheleth pauses in his whispered recitation. The word *vanity* troubles him. Maybe the word *futility* would be better. At least he is pleased with the lines about the perpetual transit of the sun. Over the years, he has conversed with many scholars in this hall, some coming from where the sun rises and sets, far beyond the boundaries of all the known kingdoms—Koheleth's reputation having been transported along the dusty trade routes by talkative Hebrew merchants who passed on tales of his intellectual exploits and proverbs as if they were valuable commodities. He suspects that the merchants embellished the tales, mixing them with news on the price of sword blades, mustard seed, and silver bangles; spicing them with warnings of bandits in the northern passes, and rumors of suspected poisonings at the Alexandrian court of Ptolemy II Philadelphus.

Some scholars had sought him on the basis of his proverbs alone, many of which he readily admitted he had not written but only collected, such as, "*the fool folds his hands and eats his own flesh.*" Or the often quoted, "*better a handful with quiet than two handfuls with toil and a chasing after wind.*" That proverb had even been inscribed on clay tablets for sale in the marketplace. Other sages had heard of his legal decisions wherein justice and mercy balanced on the thin edge of a knife blade—the rights of the poor widow being equal to the rights of a king. Although some of his visitors were gifted with the ability to listen and discern, many were entranced by their own ideas glittering like fool's gold in a streambed. Then there were the malicious few who were like slow-acting poison, tasteless and colorless, attempting to destroy Koheleth's work while appearing to support it.

Which brings him to "*nothing, nothing, all is nothing.*" He rejects that word immediately as too easy to misunderstand, verging on cynicism. *Nothing*—neither his deep dissatisfaction with the words he has available, nor the antagonism those words have sometimes stirred up—reduces life to *nothing*. Koheleth is not bitter about his declining health or regretful of the numerous failures in his long life, although he has to admit to himself that certain painful memories, springing unbidden into his mind, have the strength to make him gasp afresh at his capacity for foolishness.

He strokes the handle of his walking stick, his old reliable friend. There is beauty in it, polished smooth by the long slow pressure of his hand. When he was eleven or twelve, Koheleth had longed for wings; not the utilitarian feathers of the little brown sparrow nesting peacefully in the eaves outside his window, but the majestic plumage of the eagle, able to ride storm winds. With such powerful wings, Koheleth had dreamed of rising above the confining walls of Jerusalem, becoming a speck in the blue heavens, soaring over exotic lands only rumored to exist; following the course of a muddy river meandering through a dense jungle; or exploring endless plains covered by snow. Had someone offered him this walking stick then, he would have scorned it, throwing it away as worthless. Now he is profoundly grateful for it, leaning against the arm of his chair. Accompanying him everywhere since the days of his accident, it is made of acacia wood of which the Ark of the Covenant is also made. Neither has broken under the weight of his unrelenting demands, nor upbraided him for his long periods of apathetic neglect when he took them for granted.

Even Koheleth's mind has changed as the physical senses that provide it information have weakened and become unreliable. Those loyal subalterns—sight, hearing, touch, taste, smell—have served him faithfully his entire life. Yet now they doze at their posts, startled awake and confused by a sudden loud noise in the streets or a penetrating beam of light. As for the vehicle that has carried him through the world, it has become a rickety cart with a loose wheel and a bent axle, squeaking its way slowly down the road. Knee joints crack, ankles swell, skin sags, urine comes out in a thin sporadic stream. From the flea hopping on the tip of the dog's ear to the servant plowing the field, death comes to all, sometimes swiftly and too soon, sometimes slowly and too late, whereas the mourners feel more relief than sorrow. It is coming for Koheleth. He is trying to prepare, though he doubts the purity of his motives. Isn't this gathering yet one more attempt to gain at least a dust mote of immortality, an effort to make his ideas have permanence far beyond the borders of his time, even if his name is lost? *Mist, mist all is mist*—the words he will speak this evening, yet which his own actions belie. *Meaning, meaning, all is meaning*—that phrase is nearer the truth, less a striving after wind than a yearning for spirit, the yearning alone expansive enough to hold infinities.

Koheleth surveys the chamber with its low tables arranged in the shape of two large crescent moons facing each other, one rising, the other setting. On them are bowls of dates, almonds, and the last of the season's figs picked from Koheleth's own tree—a tree that has the strange ability to bear succulent fruit whether in or out of season, resting and reblooming on an unpredictable cycle not related to sun and rain, heat and cold. There are silver goblets for wine, wooden flagons for beer, even delicate china cups for tea. The cups had been brought from Samarkand, the great trading city at the eastern edge of what had once been the Persian empire before Alexander had defeated King Darius, slaughtered his army, and imposed Macedonian rule and Hellenistic ideas throughout most of the known world. As a young man, Koheleth had found the cups not in Samarkand (he never made it that far in his travels) but in a bustling market in Babylon near the Jewish academy where he was studying. Besides the cups, the merchant also had silk for sale, which Koheleth had never seen before. It was luminescent blue and brilliant red, both soft and strong. Koheleth could not resist purchasing the silk for his mother and sister and the cups for himself. When he returned to Jerusalem a year later via camel caravan, he wrapped the silk around the cups to protect them. All—silk, cups, self—arrived home safely. As for the tea, that could be obtained easily from the trading vessels that sailed on the monsoon winds across the Indian Ocean, anchoring in ports on the Red Sea.

Already several women and men recline on the cushions and rugs, talking quietly to each other, casting curious glances his way. Occasionally there is laughter, not too loud, more like a little ripple of water across the surface of a tranquil lake. He likes this sound, for it is the sound of friends who have come to a place they know well and in which they feel at home. Even the clicking of Saroruha's bronze prayer wheel rising up from the courtyard gives Koheleth a feeling of contentment. It reminds him of the tinkle of the little golden bells sewn to the hem of the high priest's robe that make known his presence.

It is early evening and a slight breeze lifts up the smell of dust—a gritty redolence marking the end of the dry season just before the coming of the rains. In the folds of their robes, the plaits of their hair, the soles of their sandals, the scholars themselves carry with them scents as diverse as their homelands: garlic, lemon, myrrh, camel dung, wood smoke. There is even a hint of saffron in the yellow robe of bald-headed Alithemata who eats a plum as he waits for the assembly to begin.

On the far side of the room stands Michal, her robe as white as her braided hair, giving Koheleth the impression of a marble column gleaming in the twilight. Fifty years before, Koheleth had glimpsed her for the first time from his chariot as she trimmed her grapevines with a curved blade—unveiled and dark-skinned. When he had stopped to inquire about the ownership of the vineyard and whether he might enter, she had answered him bluntly with the words from the Song of Solomon, *"My vineyard is private. You have a thousand vineyards."* His Michal! Koheleth smiles at the thought because the one word that can never be linked with her name is the possessive *his*. No one, least of all himself, has ever owned Michal who has always held a portion of herself secret and sacrosanct, as small as a mustard seed, as large as the firmament. She was the wife of his youth, the first love of his life, always his friend, his advisor, and more than any other title—his physician—the one who still has the power to lift from his heart the grief that sometimes threatens to crush it, not by removing it outright but by placing her own heart beside his. She was the one he had in mind when he wrote in his scroll: "*Two are better than one because they have a good reward for their toil, for if they fall, one will lift the other up. Woe to the one alone. When he falls there is no one to help.*" Just knowing she is in the room increases Koheleth's resolve to go on with his plans for the evening and the days ahead. "*A cord of three is not quickly broken.*" That phrase, gleaned from his reading of the ancient Sumerian poem about Gilgamesh, the ruler of the long-ago kingdom of Erech, could be comprehended several ways, Koheleth's favorite being two friends upheld by God, making a braid of three strands.

Yet none of Michal's roles, not even her capacity for blunt truthfulness, accounts for her presence this evening. Only her ability to read Sanskrit gives her the right to be here, because this is a gathering of translators summoned by Koheleth to provide guidance on his scroll. He is concerned that he may have used some words that are untranslatable into other languages. Having written many proverbs, he has a tendency to compress language, coiling as much meaning as possible into a tight spring. Before it is too late, he must ask for guidance. And he must be willing to make changes—if he has enough time.

Besides Michal, there is Targitaos from the Scythian plains where they drink the milk of mares; Dreela from the one-eyed race that lives near the gold-guarding griffins; Hemlinsu, a woman trained as a man who dresses in voluminous pants, speaking a language with two forms, one used by females, the other by males; Radeek, a throat-singer from the cold steppes a lunar-year distant.

In their midst stands a small boy, a recently purchased slave whose language is a peculiar mix of clicks and chirps, sometimes sounding like a chorus of insects on a hot night; at other times like the call of a lonesome bird. Koheleth hadn't intended to purchase him. His household staff was already too large and none of them were slaves, being paid fairly for their labor, although it had not always been so. He had meant to purchase an ancient scroll brought to Jerusalem by a trading caravan from somewhere near Sheba. However, as he and the trader were haggling over the price of the scroll, the trader had thrown the boy into the bargain. Koheleth had accepted, much to his surprise. And so while his servant had carried the scroll, Koheleth, oddly elated, had walked home leading the boy by the hand.

The boy has light brown skin, not as dark as the skin of the people far south of Elephantine downstream from the first cataract of the Nile; but neither does he look Ethiopian. His face and hands are fine-boned, his nose narrow, almost delicate. As Koheleth gazes at him, the passage in the eighteenth chapter of Isaiah comes to mind about the kingdom of Cush inhabited by *"a people tall and smooth-skinned, dreaded near and far, a people of strange speech whose land is divided by rivers."* Was he from there? Until the boy learns to speak Hebrew, there is no way to know. Ruefully, Koheleth realizes he has not been able to attend the boy's Hebrew lessons the past week, leaving the task of teaching to Michal who already treats him as if he were a member of the family. Truth is, so does Koheleth. Something about the child has brought back to him memories of his dead son who also sang softly to himself when he was playing alone. Perhaps the child has stirred the same memories in Michal, although she has not mentioned them to Koheleth. But then, when have they had the time to talk about the child, or anything else? Remorse sweeps over him as he shifts his gaze from the child to Michal who is looking back at him. She smiles and it is like the soothing balm of Gilead to his soul, flooding him with the awareness that she shares responsibility for the boy, which is the reason that she has made an effort to have him with them this evening when by all logic he should be in bed.

Counting the child, forty scholars now sit before Koheleth, chosen for their linguistic abilities combined with their awareness of the limitations of all language: not *meaning* so much as *approximations* of *meaning*, not the perfect word but the adequate word, the one that will suffice. And again the phrase a *striving after wind* curls up like a wisp of smoke through Koheleth's thoughts and he says to himself the words he has written: "*The wind goes to the south and veers to the north, round and round goes the wind, and on its circuits the wind returns. All streams flow to the sea, yet the sea is never full. To the place where the streams flow, there they return again.*"

Lycos arrives next, shuffling through the stone archway at the far end of the room, barely lifting his feet from the floor, led by his twelve-year-old granddaughter Sarah who accompanies him nearly everywhere. He turns his head toward the waning light of the high window and bows slightly, assuming correctly that Koheleth is seated at the head of the table. His vision is poor and his posture bent, yet he retains the weighty presence of a Hellenic scholar, a man who has seen with his own eyes the ways of the world and has maintained a keen interest in all that surrounds him, as ready to debate a passage of Torah as to quote Homer.

Koheleth is touched by Lycos's efforts to be in attendance. He knows personally how much Lycos's knees must have throbbed as he slowly climbed the stairs, the shortness of his breath necessitating him to pause every few steps, the rapid erratic pulse that has not yet begun to slow. Attendance is not mandatory for anyone. Giving orders has rarely been Koheleth's way. Lycos did not have to come, but he is one of the most dutiful people Koheleth has ever known. He would have come even if he had to be carried on a pallet. So also, many years before, he had not been required to stay in Jerusalem to teach Greek to Koheleth during the year following Koheleth's accident at the limestone quarry beneath the Hill of Ophel where he had gone to inspect the blocks to be used in the new residence of the high priest. Day after day in utter frustration at his inability to walk, hating to look at the angry scar running the full length of his thigh from his hip down to his swollen and throbbing knee, Koheleth had stared out of his window on the holy city, honey-colored beneath the strong sun, toward the temple on the mount wherein was the deep darkness of God—the boundless that chooses to be bound, the timeless that accepts the constraints of time—enveloped by the outstretched wings of the golden cherubim.

Meanwhile within the Greek texts that he studied with Lycos, another world of darkness and light opened up, so that without leaving his room, Koheleth roamed throughout the cosmos unfettered. Reading the *Iliad* and the *Odyssey*, he had entered the gates of Troy hidden inside a wooden horse; he had escaped from the bloodthirsty cyclops by disguising himself in sheepskin. Reading Herodotus, he had infiltrated the tribe of Amazons, each woman an expert with the bow; he had surveyed the country beyond the Istar River possessed by bees. For that mental liberation, he owed Lycos half a kingdom. Koheleth has already taken steps to guarantee that Lycos's granddaughter will have the opportunity to become a scholar in her own right. But the thought of a guarantee gives Koheleth rueful pause, the only things guaranteed being sequential random events, or to put it more bluntly—time and chance.

Not present is Koheleth's first tutor in Egyptian hieroglyphs, his beloved Cahotep, who had died of the plague many years before—a hard death of a righteous man in a hard unrighteous time when bodies had piled up in the city streets. Why some were stricken and others not had always troubled Koheleth. The same end came to all, no matter how they lived their lives; the bodies of the cherished newborn and the old profligate, who had stolen from his friends and deserted his children, were thrown into the same shallow pit.

His memories of Cahotep are not all dark, on the contrary, some are so bright they have the capacity to send an optimistic jolt into an overcast mind. When Koheleth was in his twenties, he had traveled with Cahotep to the new city of Alexandria to the west of the Nile River. Founded by Alexander the Great during the time of Koheleth's grandfather, the city's growth had been rapid under the rulership of Ptolemy Soter, one of Alexander's generals. He and Cahotep had found lodging in the thriving Jewish section in the northeast part of the city. But the presence of so large a community of fellow countrymen wasn't what drew them to Alexandria. What drew them was the magnificent library the Greek scholars called bibliothekai. On its walls were carved the words "the place of the cure of the soul." There were numerous lecture halls designed like small amphitheaters with stone steps for the students to sit on. There were long porticos where scholars from all around the Western Sea walked together while debating so intensely the air around them tingled as if lightning were about to strike. There were the garden pathways along which grew medicinal herbs and flowers, some possessing such beneficent power they could reinvigorate a faltering heart; others possessing such malevolent power, they could kill an elephant that nibbled a leaf—all carefully tended by Egyptian gardeners, not for their beauty but so that they could be dried, pulverized, and measured into numerous elixirs and potions.

Best of all to Koheleth, there was the pleasure of being able to sit down undisturbed at one of the long tables and unroll a scroll selected randomly from the shelves. Like narrow highways of papyrus, the scrolls led in all directions. No one told Koheleth where to start or how to proceed. He was free to choose with no purpose other than to learn.

There was a rule in the busy seaport of Alexandria that any ship entering the harbor with scrolls onboard (whether the personal possession of the master kept for his own pleasure or official documents sent by a foreign government) had to lend them to the library to be copied before the ship would be allowed to hoist anchor and depart. It was rumored as well that the copies were of such high quality that often the library kept the originals, returning the facsimiles to the ship's master who was none the wiser. By means of this concentrated copying, the library had grown rapidly in all subjects: medicine, mathematics, astronomy, cartography, engineering. Moreover, certain scrolls, as well as some of the scholars with whom Koheleth became friends, not only revealed facts but also the methods to measure and test them, breaking things down into their component parts, then putting them together again, all of which pointed to an orderliness underlying the natural world.

One of his new friends was a young man named Euclid who already had the reputation of a great scholar. He and Koheleth walked along the library porticos discussing the ideas of Eudoxus, particularly his method to determine areas and volumes bounded by curves. Mathematics was not an area in which Koheleth excelled; nevertheless, he was attracted to it as he was to many subjects beyond his grasp, their difficulty being part of their attraction. Euclid had set for himself the task of codifying all the geometry then known among the Greeks and Egyptians, putting it together so that students could learn in a systematic way. It was Euclid's clear organization and deductive methodology based on self-evident axioms and postulates that most impressed Koheleth. Euclid read as broadly as the library would allow, which was as broadly as the world would allow. Furthermore, he had consulted with numerous sources, not just written, including Egyptian priests who were not normally forthcoming with information they considered arcane and sacred. The Greeks—who had a much looser relationship with their deities, considering them to be on the verge of irrelevant—treated mathematics and geometry as secular, despite the fact that they pointed to a beautiful all-encompassing order in the universe. Euclid's work had removed the vestiges of magic, showing why, for example, the interior angles of all triangles added up to two right angles. He had demonstrated to Koheleth that there wasn't anything miraculous about mathematics. This meant that it was comprehensible to everyone who was willing to learn, not only the intelligent males of the upper class who had the time to dally over such things, but also the local carpenter and the sea captain. Koheleth could see Euclid's point, but it didn't stop him from arguing vehemently that there was also disorder in the universe, something far beyond the postulates, having to do with unpredictability, uncorrelated possibilities, and mathematical inconsistency.

It was not all serious debate. Euclid was also good company, great for a lively evening at the tavern, quick with the quip, the humorous answer, the memorable phrase, being famous for having responded to Ptolemy—who, like so many mediocre students, wanted to know if there were a shortcut to understanding instead of having to actually do the calculations—that "there is no royal road to geometry." And indeed there was not. The knowledge could only be gained the hard way.

Koheleth could have spent his entire life in Alexandria. However, Cahotep, who had been hired by Koheleth's father to advance the young man's knowledge of all things, knew that *"of making many scrolls there is no end, and much study is wearisome to the flesh,"* (as Koheleth would eventually write in his scroll). So one night when Koheleth had imbibed too much cheap wine in a tavern frequented by the younger scholars, Cahotep had hustled him onto a boat heading down the channel that connected Alexandria to the Nile. When Koheleth awoke next morning, his head pounding like a hammer against an anvil, the soft lapping of water against the hull was his first inkling that something was amiss. But his fury at finding that Alexandria had disappeared upriver was quickly quenched by the wonders of Memphis and Thebes wherein pyramids of great antiquity were surrounded by thriving marketplaces filled with exotic foods and spices brought by boat via the Red Sea and by camel caravans across the desert. To Koheleth, the pyramids were a disconcerting marvel, calling into question the claim of the Hebrews that theirs was one of the oldest civilizations on Earth. Even if Koheleth's ancestor Joseph had gone down to Egypt four hundred years before the birth of Moses, the land wherein he rose to power as an advisor to the pharaoh was already ancient.

When the pyramids and ruins had been thoroughly climbed and studied (including a session with a local practitioner on embalming techniques and another with a builder on the method of moving large stone blocks great distances), Koheleth and Cahotep had headed south, joining a caravan on its way to the walled city of Sheba, hot as a kiln, the place of legend mentioned in the Torah, ruled by sixty queens until the time of

King Solomon. Cahotep was so overweight from his love of food and wine he bounced up and down on the back of the camel like a round berry, his short legs useless for balance. Chortling at his discomfort, he kept calling out the name of his own long-suffering donkey waiting for him back in Jerusalem, and cursing the refractory camel all in the same breath, much to the delight of the camel drivers, who benefitted not only from Cahotep's self-deprecating sense of humor but from his largesse with tips. Cahotep knew how to travel, which was to use money whenever it would smooth out what could humanly be smoothed, and if that were not possible, to make the most of whatever befell him, finally resorting to heartfelt prayer not just to one deity but to several, in case the first wasn't listening, and the second and third were ill-disposed to help. The trip across the Red Sea was an example. They had embarked on a rickety teak boat of the spice trade, smelling of cinnamon, which sat so low in the water it was in danger of swamping. When a thunderstorm had swept down on them, Cahotep had implored Elohim the entire way across to part the waters just once more, as he had done for the Hebrews, so that Cahotep could walk on dry ground. Then he had intoned a chant to Poseidon in case he should suddenly find himself a denizen of his kingdom, and finally for good measure, he had prayed to Anquet, the Egyptian water goddess.

The prospects of sinking were indeed dire even to Koheleth who, like most young men, was energized by the presence of danger. Fortunately, they had safely reached the land of frankincense and myrrh where they had visited a marble obelisk on which the history of the Sabaean rulers was carved, or so they were told by the locals, not being able to read the words themselves. On the base of one of the obelisks, Koheleth had scratched his own name along with the word *here*. As Koheleth knelt in the hot sand with a chisel, Cahotep roared with laughter wondering about what future scholars would conclude on discovering a Hebrew name scratched into a plinth just off the Incense Road far south of Sinai.

Koheleth smiles to himself when he realizes that he is attempting to do exactly the same thing with his scroll. Now an old man, he has substituted a pen for the chisel, vellum for stone, but his message is the same as it had been when he was young: Koheleth was here; he existed; he mattered. Koheleth remembers that it was during that trip (in fact, as a direct result of his graffiti) that Cahotep had come up with the intriguing idea of cutting different languages into a single stone stele in the hope that people in the future would be able to parse the meaning of the passage if, by some unfortunate chance, all knowledge of one or two of the individual languages had been lost; for example, including hieroglyph with Egyptian Demotic and Greek, all of which Cahotep could write with ease. It was a concern Koheleth shared, because Aramaic and Persian were already mixing with Hebrew, and the way he wrote differed from the way the scribe of Genesis wrote. This truth was underscored by a little clay seal he had in his possession, cylindrical in shape, apparently from a culture that no longer existed. It had been brought back to Judah by one of his ancestors who had been born in Babylon during the Great Captivity a few centuries earlier. Perhaps used to identify ownership in an ancient time, the seal appeared to have on it a form of writing that was not pictographic; yet for all Koheleth's efforts, he had been unable to decipher it. It had forced him to conclude that languages could die. The needs of a kingdom shifted, traders brought strange words, and conquerors forced the conquered to speak in strange tongues. That had been the fate of his ancestors who could barely speak Hebrew upon their return from exile to Jerusalem, a city they had never seen. Nothing was fixed, yet all things stayed the same. On the one hand, languages were as permanent as the Sea of Galilee, and on the other, as ephemeral as a vernal pond in the Engedi.

    Koheleth turns his thoughts back to the sages filing into the room just as Cahotep's much younger successor Djadao enters. He is not watching where he is going, concentrating instead on an unusual palm leaf that he holds in his hand. Koheleth knows what it is because he was the one who gave it to him, having purchased it from a Nabatean trader who in his far-flung trips to the east kept a look-out for odd things. Only in his round physical shape is Djadao like Cahotep, being to Koheleth a bit tedious in his fascination with creation myths, always comparing Moses to child deities arising from rivers, and pointing out the commonality of flood narratives across cultures. He also tends to over-concentrate on his studies, losing touch with everything around him, dwelling not in the present world but in prior worlds glimpsed through things such as this very beautiful leaf. When Koheleth talks to Djadao, he is never sure where Djadao's mind is in chronological time. Koheleth considers it a failing: to become so wrapped up in work that one is not aware of the hardship such a level of concentration imposes on family, servants, and friends; to lose all sense of balance, not taking the time to taste an aged wine or to sit quietly with a friend. To be truthful, it is a failing that Koheleth shares with Djadao and for which Michal has had to sternly upbraid him, on many occasions taking him by the hand and pulling him out of his library into the full light of day to watch his children (and now his grandchildren) play.

Koheleth wonders if Djadao will ever gain the patience to become wise. His patience, what there is of it, is forced, as evidenced by his physical restlessness and a drift of his gaze when he becomes bored with a conversation. Even so, Koheleth has to admit that the palm leaf Djadao is studying is worth his single-minded attention because it bears on its veined surface a strange script written in an exquisite calligraphy that indicates the culture from which it comes has a professional class of scribes. He wonders if the language is similar to Hebrew wherein each letter is holy, capable of dancing in the air alone, scattering precursors of meaning that sprout into words and bloom into sentences. Koheleth had questioned the Nabatean trader, but he did not know anything about the leaf's origins, having bartered for it from another trader who came from yet another civilization even further to the east, somewhere on that trade route that was said to finally end in a land ruled by red dragons breathing fire.

Koheleth wishes that his life could be extended so that he might travel that route to see for himself if the fantastic stories were true, but even now, as he waits for everyone to arrive, he feels weighed down as if he were wearing a robe woven of iron threads. Occasionally his heart beats so fast within his chest, he becomes dizzy and the air around him seems inadequate, as if he were being held against his will under water. He lies down at night fatigued and arises at dawn even more fatigued. Fortunately, at the moment, Koheleth's heart is quiet, for which he is thankful because he is about to put it under great strain. Djadao being the last of the translators on his staff to enter the room, Koheleth now must use one of his most unusual abilities to summon more people to him. Quoting from Psalm 19 written by King David, he whispers: "*Day to day declares speech, night to night proclaims knowledge. No voice, no words, unheard the sound, yet voices go forth in all the earth and world without end.*"

As he finishes intoning the lines from the psalm, other scholars begin to enter through the arches, speaking unknown tongues: Ega sung beyond the Pillars of Hercules, Dzongkha spoken in a kingdom so high its ruler claims ownership of the clouds, and Haudenosaunee, a language heard across an immensity of water. Most of these languages have no alphabets and, therefore, cannot be written on papyrus, animal skins, palm leaves, or stone. There is a woman from the jungle whose language has no means of counting. Near her walks another woman with red hair who can only speak in present tense but whose head position indicates past or future. They are followed by a man whose language has no words for color, although he himself is dressed in a rainbow-hued robe that reminds Koheleth of the story of his ancestor Joseph and his splendid coat. If Koheleth were to ask him, would the scholar respond that he is dressed in woven plant fiber dyed with powdered sea snail and pulverized beetle? Would his description not be more accurate than bluish-purple and red? Even more peculiar, there are some languages from the distant future that cannot be spoken at all, being instead immense patterns of the numbers one and two.

By the time they have all gathered in the upper room, so many languages are sparking on and off in the lavender darkness, they are like fireflies on a warm summer night, ineffable codes held aloft by fragile wings. Words words words. No end of them. A murmur, a babble, each speaker trying to understand the other, listening for any sound that might align with some word they already know, providing the unlocking key. Koheleth is the only one to understand all. Again he smiles inwardly at his overdrawn assessment of himself. What is the difference between a fool and a sage? A sage is certain he is a fool while a fool is certain he is a sage. A sage grows humbler with age, a fool grows prouder. What other certainties can Koheleth claim to know? First, that most of what he plans to say this evening and in the coming days will be misunderstood and eventually forgotten. Second, that in some places his words may be banned or considered either irreverent or irrelevant. No matter what happens, it is out of his hands, yet he acts as if he has control. Resignedly, Koheleth makes a gesture to his servant to light the oil lamps on the tables. As the burning reed touches each wick, a shadow play appears on the walls. Here, a lifted wine goblet. There, a hand gesturing. Because it is the time of year just after the festival of Sukkot, Koheleth uses the traditional words used to greet mysterious guests, "Be seated, guests from on high, be seated! Be seated, guests of faith, be seated!" By the time the last lamp is lit, everyone has found a place to sit and the room has grown quiet.

Koheleth waits while the silence thickens, enveloping the scholars like a prayer shawl, calming them down. A little brown bat flutters in one window and out the other, his rapid wing-beats the only sound. Koheleth knows that the bat has ways of seeing and hearing that can penetrate the darkness. He prays that in the days to come he will be similarly endowed.

He holds up his hands. "Welcome." All eyes turn his way. "I have never been able to follow my own advice, which is: *let your words be few*," he begins. There is laughter, unmuffled and full, from all his friends. In the rafters there is a Boolean twitter. "To ease the task of translating my final work, I have gathered you together to go over the draft from the beginning." Around the table, there is the sound of scrolls being unrolled and of cushions being moved closer together. In the shadow of the arch, there is a slight whirling of lights followed by a soft hum. Koheleth pauses and takes a deep breath, choosing his words. *"Mist, mist, all is mist. What does man gain from all his labor, toiling under the sun? Generations go and generations come, and the earth stays forever."*

2

Striving After Wind

"Let us consider the Hebrew word *hevel*, meaning variously *vapor, worthlessness, futility, mist, nothingness, fog, emptiness,* and *breath*. Of them all, I prefer the word *mist*. Beautiful when thin rays of sunlight reach through. Dangerous when it conceals, causing a person to become disoriented or to stumble. *Mist* beckons silently, almost alive in the way it moves, as if gray fingers are slowly stirring the current of a gray river."

"Even though it causes a person, such as yourself, to stumble, I think the word *mist* is better than *miasma* or *haze*—two other possibilities, negative in their connotations," says Michal, looking up from the partially unrolled scroll at the opposite end of the table from Koheleth. "The first: swamp vapor smelling of rotting vegetation. The second: an obscuring dullness caused by smoke from a distant fire or sand from a storm in the desert." Michal's comment about Koheleth stumbling is spoken with the hint of affectionate jest, for he has the dubious reputation of either wandering in thought without taking note of his surroundings or of being so observant of some singular phenomenon, such as the orange bristles on the back of a caterpillar chewing the leaves of an orange lily, that he overlooks not only the lily itself but also the hoe left lying on the ground by the gardener.

"Might as well use *gloomy*—another possibility in which sound and sense converge." Into Koheleth's mind springs an image of craggy highlands fissured by dark ravines overshadowed by scudding gray clouds. A cold shiver, like a premonition, runs through his body. "No, it will not do. Perhaps the word *cloudy*," he asks tentatively, bending his head slightly to the side and pressing his lips together as if negating the suggestion even as he is making it. "Except that a person can still see what is in front of him on a cloudy day unless he is actually *in* the cloud."

"Did not God appear on Mt. Sinai as a cloud that Moses had to enter to receive the ten words, later known as the Ten Commandments?" asks Lycos, his voice gravelly with age, making the other sages bend towards him to hear. His question is rhetorical because he knows the answer full well, being as versed in the Hebrew texts as he is in the Greek. "Did not that same cloud lead your ancestors day by day out of the fleshpots of Egypt into this bountiful land flowing with milk and honey? And what is a cloud if not mist? What is mist if not water that is in the air, eventually to become rain that falls on the dry land, making the wheat seed sprout, giving us bread to eat?"

"The answers are yes, yes, yes, and yes, if I counted your questions correctly," comments Targitaos dryly. The Socratic style of debate that Lycos loves to use, constantly interrogating his listeners, annoys him, the Scythian style being much more direct, at times resorting to weapons to settle a point or, if diplomacy is needed, analyzing the steaming entrails of a goat, slit open on the council floor, for what they portend.

"Then I will add a fifth question," retorts Lycos amicably, knowing that this is a longstanding game between himself and Targitaos that they both like to play. His questioning pomposity is an opening gambit, a verbal flourish to start the action and nothing more. "Did not God require the Hebrews to wait in camp whenever the cloud hovered over the tabernacle? And the answer is, of course, a fifth yes. They were not to rush around trying to dissipate the mist, complaining of its vaporous opacity. They were simply to wait watchfully until the cloud lifted. So, Targitaos, do you have a better word?"

"Another question! Six! No, not a better word, just a different one mentioned by Koheleth already: *fog*. I think it would suffice—and note my use of the word *suffice*. The trouble with fog is that I doubt all lands experience it, so I am not sure of its universality—one of the criteria that Koheleth has set for his scroll and that we must keep in mind over the next few days. I have seen heavy fog in the desert but only along the coast. Fog is also more enclosing, even impenetrable, whereas the word mist implies something lighter, less ominous. Objects and ideas can be glimpsed through mist." Targitaos is not sitting at the table but against the wall beneath a window. Because he wears a black robe and a large black turban wrapped low on his brow, his craggy face, dimly illuminated, seems to float in the air as if disembodied.

"Nor is *fog* inherently negative as are most of the alternatives Koheleth has listed for meanings of *hevel*, such as *emptiness* and *nothingness*," adds Michal who, dressed all in white, is a gleaming foil to Targitaos, although in temperament they are more like twins—serious, blunt, and slightly aloof. And yet often there is about Michal's face the expectancy of a smile, hinted in the slight upturn of the corners of her mouth and the tiny twinkle in her eyes, as if a good idea or a warm memory had just come to mind but had not been expressed.

"How can *emptiness* be negative?" asks Alithemata turning toward Michal. He cups his hands together as if to hold water, then lifts them up to the level of his chin, his fingers so bent with age that if water from a pitcher were to be poured into them, it would cascade through the gaping cracks, splash down onto his round belly and run over his thighs. "As the Heart Sutra says, form is emptiness; emptiness is form. The space between my right and left hands does not exist independently from the skin, muscle, and bone of my palms."

Alithemata's response is no surprise to Koheleth. The two men have been friends for many decades, ever since on a whim Koheleth purchased Alithemata as a slave, fascinated by his bald head, strange yellow attire, and imperturbable visage. A prize of war between two eastern kingdoms, Alithemata had been traded to slavers. By the time they had brought him to the slave market of Jerusalem—where he sat cross-legged, surveying the scene as if he were the one making a selection—the traders were well aware of Alithemata's worthlessness as a laborer, not having any fear of pain and death to compel him to be cooperative. But they hoped that they could recoup their investment by selling him to someone, such as Koheleth, as a kind of cultural curiosity, much like one of the top-knotted and perfumed eunuchs who served as decoration in the quarters of the concubines. Whatever were Koheleth's reasons for purchasing Alithemata, he quickly forgot them when he discovered that Alithemata's comprehension of languages was immense and his understanding of esoteric beliefs, such as transmigration and reincarnation, even more immense. As a result, Koheleth had freed him shortly after purchase and had offered him a position on his staff, which was then quite small, comprised only of Lycos and Cahotep. Alithemata had refused, returning instead to his home in the east, only to come back to Jerusalem two years later, this time on his own volition, and for good. Never once had Koheleth rued his impetuous decision to purchase a man who could not be purchased that day in the slave market.

Despite his poor eyesight, Koheleth observes the wall behind Alithemata as he speaks. He sees wavering shadows caused by the blocking of light by Alithemata's hands. The light comes from the lamps that are hollow receptacles holding oil. By the end of the evening, the oil will be gone, and the flames will sputter out in wisps of smoke. "In Genesis, the earth is without *form* and *void*. Empty," reflects Koheleth. "And like the Bodhisattva Avalokitesvara moving in the deep way of Wisdom, God's spirit hovers over the emptiness of the abyss. I have considered using the word."

"The problem with emptiness is that it can be misunderstood. You do not want readers to conclude that the search for wisdom is a waste of time," Michal replies in a matter-of-fact way, stressing the last phrase, "particularly young readers and scholars who might think that you are telling them that learning anything at all is pointless. Life itself—pointless!"

"For the same reason, watch out how you use absolutes, such as mist *all* is mist, or emptiness *all* is emptiness," interjects Lycos.

"Even so, I wish I could use the word emptiness." Koheleth hesitates, leaning his head back and peering into the darkness outside the window. "I am trying to convey a state in which everything is in flux, not this, not that, like water droplets suspended in air, not yet rain, not yet snow. As I have written, '*round and round goes the wind and on its circuits the wind returns*.'"

"So you have an invisible force—the wind—traveling on an invisible circuit that does not exist until the force follows it," muses Alithemata. "If emptiness can be compounded, you have done so."

Michal leans in emphatically as the flame of the lamp in front of her momentarily flares and the golden light flickers across Alithemata's shiny bald head. "Most of the people who will read this scroll will not possess your understanding of emptiness. To them it will mean worthless. And that will make the recitation of this passage into a dirge. How terrible it will be if someone condemned to death recites *emptiness, emptiness* in the final moments of his misspent and misunderstood life."

"Or, even worse, if that condemned person intones those words at the end of a *well*-spent and *well*-understood life," breaks in Targitaos. "As to the idea of wasting time, I would like to add that Lycos's point made a few minutes ago about watchful waiting should not be lost in this discussion. It is an important one." And Targitaos looks toward Lycos in a gesture of conciliation that Lycos acknowledges with a slight nod of his head.

"Yes," says Alithemata very quietly. "Sometimes mind must wait for soul." The sound of his voice vibrates through the hall like the harmonics of a temple bell after it has been struck. "The mind is fast, the soul is slow; the first is a torrent tumbling down the mountain, the second is the mountain." With his hands, Alithemata mimics the speed of the water followed by the almost imperceptible creep of the earth, concluding by folding his hands in his lap, and bowing slightly with his head, indicating to Koheleth and Michal that he is done speaking.

Koheleth is not surprised by the swiftness and intensity with which the discussion has begun, because everyone who has spoken thus far knows each other well. Essentially, they are carrying on a long-running conversation or, to be more truthful, debate, one person's practicality serving to balance another's mysticism. What concerns Koheleth is whether the strangers in the room will take part. His friends' ideas are important, but Koheleth is more interested in hearing from the woman dressed in white fur who is sitting with her back against one of the columns, or the man with the conical reed hat who crouches at the top of the stairs smoking a long clay pipe, occasionally blowing smoke rings into the room. It is not by Koheleth's own power that they have been summoned from the realms of awe to sit together this evening in Jerusalem; and it is not by his own power that they are able to decipher the scroll. In fact, the only power Koheleth now possesses is the ability to watchfully wait, as Lycos and Targitaos have mentioned. Something is going to happen. As it is written in Isaiah, he has prepared the way and made straight the paths. Now his job is similar to that of a night watchman standing at the door of the temple.

"You should use the word *vanity*," chirps Kish, another old friend who perches, rather than sits, to Koheleth's left. An expert in the language of birds, Kish's words undulate through the air like the flight of a little goldfinch. Iridescent green feathers from a quetzal rise from his headpiece. The indigo feathers of a macaw are sewn onto his tunic. On his arm is the tattoo of an eagle, its talons drawn in such a way that they appear to be gripping Kish's muscle.

"I used *vanity* in several earlier drafts, ultimately deleting it and substituting *mist*. But *vanity* can be taken to mean vapid pride—a pride not warranted by a person's words or deeds."

"Which makes it all the more appropriate," asserts Kish, the last word sounding like the clicking of a beak on a thistle seed. "A prideful person suffers from self-imposed blindness; a misty veil over his eyes. No matter where all of us come from," and Kish waves his hand in a full circle indicating everyone in the room, "I am certain that we have all known rulers and chiefs who were so proud of their achievements they presumed they knew the right course of action in every circumstance: refusing to take the advice of honest counselors; using tax money and conscription to build themselves palaces; making war on peaceable neighbors for no purpose but personal glory; in time of famine demanding for themselves the most succulent meat from a depleted herd while the children starve. *Vanity, vanity, all is vanity,* that is how it should read, for all things are a striving after wind." Kish swivels his head like a hawk and peers at everyone in a piercing way that reduces them all to the size of plump mice about to be eaten for dinner. The silence that envelops the room is like that of a jungle gone eerily quiet. "I have seen a proud tribe of people turned into wanderers without even a pot to claim as their own, all because of *vanity* and a striving after wind." Kish says the words with vehemence then stops abruptly as if the memory is as constricting as a fishing line tangled around the neck of a cormorant.

"What means this *striving after wind* that you say as if you cannot swallow?" The question comes from the second circle behind those seated at the table. Lithe in appearance, the questioner has black hair pulled into a single braid to which is tied the tawny tip of a mountain lion's tail. He speaks softly with pauses between each word as if he is taking them out, one by one, from different leather pouches and setting them carefully in a row.

"Please speak a little louder and tell us your name," says Koheleth encouragingly, leaning toward the man and cupping his left ear with his hand. "There are many old ears in this room, mine included." The man stands up and steps into a circle of light cast by one of the lamps and as he does so, Koheleth notices that he wears draped over his shoulder a mantle of animal skin covered with the purple shells of the channeled whelk. Suddenly the word *wampum* springs into Koheleth's mind, a word he has never heard before. Such mental intrusions have been occurring with increasing frequency. He thinks of them as little honeybees that flit through his brain carrying on their fuzzy bodies the pollen of other languages; or, if he is out of sorts, he thinks of them as pesky mosquitoes buzzing in his ears, or dusky moths fluttering against the inside of his skull. He waves his hand as if to whisk this particular insect away, but the word *wampum* continues to hum. Koheleth hopes he will get the opportunity later on to take a closer look at the mantle. He wonders whether the arrangement of the shells might be a kind of writing, a way to chronicle important events, similar to the use of intricate knots tied in string. Do the purple shells indicate the sounds of consonants and vowels? Do the patterns move from left to right? up and down? or like the sunflower, do they spiral? Koheleth has never been able to stop himself from asking questions of all he sees, and even on this most important evening, he finds he must rein in his unruly mind. The questions for the man about his wampum mantle will have to wait.

Gazing over the gathering, the man begins again, louder this time but with a melodic intonation that, while pleasing to the ear, requires the close attention of the sages. "I am Ayonwentah. To speak your language instead of Haudenosaunee pierces tongue with a thorn. But I try: what means this *striving after wind*?"

"Chasing after something useless, trying to catch the air in your fists," Koheleth explains, making the motion of grabbing something with his hand, then slowly opening his clenched fingers to show nothing.

"Oh," says Ayonwentah. "Oh," he repeats, sounding like an owl calling from its perch in a tall tree as twilight thickens in the forest. He pauses to consider Koheleth's explanation and to gather his thoughts into an expressible form. "Then to my people *striving after wind*" —and he makes exactly the same gesture as Koheleth has done—"means the opposite of what it means to you. Good not bad. Four winds carry powerful messages from the spirit world to which we must listen. Even though we build long houses and plant gardens, we do not stay in one place. We are wanderers, *wind strivers*, our direction set by the seasonal movement of animals and birds, the shellfish on the shore, the ripening of fruit in the fall, the rising of sap in sugar maples at the end of winter. Nor does *to strive after wind* mean to attempt something hopeless. It means to be perceptive of the spirits calling to us out of the north, south, east, west. They do not call clearly; instead they whisper in the marsh grass or ride on a slanting beam of light, through dreams, visions." As if he is himself a vision, Ayonwentah seems to waver and grow dim as he steps out of the circle of light and sits back down into the semi-darkness.

"We have barely begun this discussion and already you and Kish have cut to the bone marrow, which is the ambiguous nature of words, made more so by the use of metaphor that cannot leap the chasm between cultures and times," replies Koheleth, envisioning a vast canyon that only an eagle could cross. "For example, our Hebrew poets often speak of God as a solitary shepherd and his people as a flock of sheep. One of our kings wrote, 'The Lord is my shepherd I shall not want. He makes me lie down in green pastures. He leads me beside still waters.' But that means nothing to people who have never seen a flock of sheep and who do not know of their tendency to follow each other without thought, even to their own harm. Would your family, Ayonwentah, think that a flock of sheep is like a herd of bison, so enormous and powerful that the pounding of their hooves in a stampede sounds like thunder rolling across the prairie?" Koheleth pauses briefly, startled by the clarity of the image in his mind of shaggy brown beasts he has never seen running by the thousands over a grassy plain he has never visited. As did the word *wampum*, the image has come unbidden. "Or you, Kish, in your jungle, would your people envision a troop of monkeys screaming in the treetops and throwing down overripe fruit on the head of a man foolish enough to attempt to herd them with a crooked staff in one hand and a rod in the other?"

"Even in Hebrew the metaphor of the shepherd and the sheep can be taken in several ways, positive and negative," interjects Djadao. He scoops up a handful of almonds from a bowl on the table and puts them in his mouth, chewing as he talks. "If you are a sheep, does the good shepherd plan to shear you and use your wool? Or eat you for dinner? Is he leading you beside still waters only for your benefit? Or for his?"

"You are asking what is in the valley of the shadow of death for the sacrificial lamb! An astute question that upends the metaphor." Koheleth intentionally ignores the slightly sarcastic tone of Djadao's voice. He lifts his cup of wine and takes a drink, then gazes into its dark red depth as if the answer might be floating just below the surface. "Which shows that the most perfect translation we are capable of achieving is at best misleading. Language is the greatest gift of God to humankind, yet I also fear it. And fear *for* it. It is the easiest gift to use and misuse; the first word is a blessing, the second a curse."

Koheleth turns to Kish who is sitting by his side and makes a conciliatory gesture with his hand as if smoothing ruffled feathers. "Kish, in arguing for the word *vanity*, you mentioned taxes and conscription. It is possible that the only writing that will be understandable in a thousand years are lists of numbers and names: 'paid to pharaoh 1000 amphorae of wine, 1000 bushels of wheat, 100 men for 100 days to work on the pyramid.' And will anyone remember who the pharaoh was, let alone the 100 men whose bone-crushing labor built a memorial long fallen into decay in memory of nothing and no one?"

Kish begins to tap a rhythm on the table with the nail of his right index finger, making the sound of a small woodpecker seeking an insect in a dead tree trunk. "All of us would like words to be rocks that we can set in one immovable place. That is why rulers have their images sculpted in stone, and why some people have their names or symbols scratched into cave walls when they die. But words flow like the sap in trees, rising up into other words, branching out into yet more words. The life of the language is in change as is all life. And is that bad? You write in your scroll that all rivers run to the sea but the sea is never full. What if it were full? Then the rivers would stop flowing, the cycle of birth and death would end, and there would be silence. No tapping of the woodpecker." Kish stops tapping. "No bird song." Kish stops talking. It is as if a goldfinch has fallen out of the air, dead.

"The word in my universe for that branching is *fractal*, wherein the Hausdorff-Besicovitch dimension is greater than the topological dimension," comes a voice from above the wooden rafters, more felt than heard as if the membranes of the mind have been set to vibrating instead of the eardrums.

Koheleth looks up into the domain of darkness from which the vibration seems to emanate. "Can you speak in more—how shall I say it?" and instantly the phrase *user-friendly language* slips from Koheleth's mouth like a bee zooming through an open door. From the vibration comes a soft clattering as of little squares being depressed sequentially by fingers.

"A fractal is a recurring pattern, in which the branches replicate the source, easy to calculate rapidly by computer."

"A computer?" asks Djadao, incredulous that something or someone is speaking to the assembly from the direction of the ceiling. "Do you mean a *person* who counts, or a *thing* that counts?"

"Person, thing, the same." There is a halt, then a hum. "To clarify, a computer is a mechanical device based on algorithms, which in this case has allowed me to query: if not *vanity*, what about the word *meaningless*?"

"Meaningless to whom?" Koheleth is in a quandary. If he is to acquiesce to the idea that something not human is addressing him, and he is addressing it, must he also acquiesce to the idea that what the words *mind* and *intelligence* signify is disputable? Not having enough lifetimes, let alone seconds, to come up with an answer, he decides on the spur of the moment to address the invisible thing with the same respect he accords to humans. "I myself do not understand algorithms as thoroughly as I should. However, there are people in this room who understand them supremely well. Perhaps that is true of *you*—if I may use the pronoun for the second-person-singular as a form of address. To this day, though I hate to admit it, even the simple idea of zero as an actual physical entity eludes me. What is its meaning? As I write a little further on in this first chapter, '*what is not there cannot be counted.*' But

I know full well that the lack of apparent meaning is only an indication of my own limitations. The zero is not to blame."

"Two plus two yields an answer. The ratio of the circumference of the circle to its diameter yields an infinite answer. My language is algorithmic. It yields billions of answers. Mathematics provides *answers,* not *meaning,* by which is implied purpose. Everything is process, hence without purpose. Everything is numbers. Ergo, humans are numbers."

"I see you are an old Pythagorean, my new—friend." Koheleth hesitates on the last word. "Since I disagree with the Pythagoreans, at least on certain points, I must by logic disagree with you on the nature of humans. Some magi contend that God thinks in numbers, may indeed *be* numbers. And in studying nature closely, as I have done, I can see their point: the six sides of the snowflake, each one different, each the same, and all exquisite; the spiral pattern of the sunflower, the florets arranged 1,1,2,3,5,8,13,21, every number the sum of the two numbers preceding it. Yet in spite of all that, I feel that there is something in a human that escapes the wheels within wheels of numbers, is undecidable by any calculation, incomplete in its self-reference. A randomness. Or, to put it as simply as I can, a human is something that does not add up. Not *less* than numbers. *More* than numbers!"

Koheleth had never had much patience with the Hebrew scholars who perceived in the Torah hidden messages from God encrypted in numbers, a practice arising naturally from the assignment of a numeric value to each letter of the alphabet, beginning with the *aleph* as one, *bet* as two. He had wasted much time with numerology early in his life (although he hadn't considered it a waste then), glorying in the challenge of seeking arcane meanings he alone was intelligent enough to decipher. A fine example of vanity and striving after wind! But then slowly he had become aware of how easy it was for him to manipulate the data, making the sum of certain letters and verses equal a desired result, either by combining two verses into one or conversely breaking one verse into two, the precise separation between verses often being a matter of conjecture. It was a stern lesson he had carried over into his other studies as well. Numerology had made him skeptical of his own thought-processes, heightening his awareness of the human tendency to fit the facts to longed-for results, of creating meaning and then presuming that the meaning was pre-existent. Koheleth turns his face to the rafters again, attempting to discern any fluctuation in air currents. "The patterns I mentioned of the snowflake and the sunflower are beautiful. The *recognition* of those patterns is a human's first task, analogous to Adam naming the animals that God had formed out of the dust; *understanding* them is the second task. What kind of patterns do your fractals make?"

"An infinity of patterns. Watch," says the voice and suddenly near the top of the far wall appears a seepage of water gathering itself into a little rivulet that begins to flow downward as if across the face of a sandbank. It branches, then branches again, and again, until the wall is transformed into what appears to be a gleaming map of an enormous river delta disgorging its water into the sea, which in this instance is the floor. Then the image vanishes and in its place a tiny white crystal emerges from the center of the wall. It begins to replicate itself, blooming outward like the fronds of a gigantic fern.

The child, who has been leaning against Alithemata's side half-asleep for most of the discussion, is now fully awake, his eyes wide and his mouth open with wonder. While all the sages are captivated by the beauty of the display, their line of work has, to a degree, inured them to the unexpected and strange. Only the child is new enough in the world to be in awe. He claps his hands in excitement and instantly the icy ferns wither and are gone, and the wall recedes into darkness. Next a little three-dimensional pinecone materializes on the table in front of the boy. He begins to reach for it with both hands but Alithemata holds him back and indicates to him to watch, for a second pinecone has begun to form on the first pinecone and on the second a third until in no time at all there is a mountain range of pinecones covering the table. The child laughs with delight and claps his hands again and in a twinkling all the pinecones are gone. He frowns in disappointment, and Alithemata pats his head in consolation.

"Please, would you do one more pattern for the child?" he asks the air, not knowing in which direction to speak. This time a single five-pointed star materializes on the ceiling, which has turned indigo blue. It hovers there alone like the first star of the evening, then at each tip another smaller star appears, and then yet a smaller one, and smaller. At first the appearance of the new stars is slow enough so that the viewers can comprehend how the pattern is evolving, but then it speeds up until the linked cluster regresses rapidly backwards at the same time that it hurtles forwards, silver and gold against blue, giving the illusion that the ceiling has disappeared, replaced by the heavens.

"It is infinite, isn't it?" gasps Koheleth in amazement. "What seems to be out-of-line is actually in-line. I have asked the question in my scroll whether the crooked can be made straight."

"I shall look it up for you on the internet," hums the voice in flat intonation as the stars disappear and the ceiling returns to normal. "The crooked and the straight are in the Pythagorean table of opposites; one is needed for the other to exist."

You are not only a good Pythagorean, but a good Buddhist!" chortles Koheleth. Alithemata beams with a smile that flows outward from his face, splashing first onto the boy then continuing around the table from person to person until like a rippling wave it comes full circle and subsides into Alithemata's eyes. The laughter breaks the enchantment that the fractals had cast.

The speaker in the rafters does not comprehend the humor of Koheleth's statement or the human response to it. "That does not compute, other than the dates. Siddhartha Gautama, known as the Buddha, and Pythagoras, as well as Zarathustra, also known as Zoroaster of the Persians, were born in what will be designated the sixth century before the common era, if one is to follow inaccurate human dating systems."

"The same period of time in which the Hebrews were in exile in Babylon and the Prophet Daniel hung about with lions in their den," quips Djadao.

"In support of the word *mist* instead of the word *meaningless*," interrupts Targitaos, trying to head off what appears to him to be the tangling of several threads of logic, or illogic, that will tie the entire evening in knots if allowed to continue, "it is a noun for something that occurs in nature all over the world, a sensation, a dampness on the skin, a shiver. Of all the parts of speech, a noun is the most—I hesitate to use the word—*real*. And that makes it understandable in different languages. The same is true of *wind*, also a noun."

"The wind is blowing. Adore the wind. The words of Pythagoras," drones the voice.

"Please, may I continue?" Targitaos asks with barbed politeness.

"Is your power source adequate? Is your program functioning properly?"

Targitaos stares up at the ceiling with a look that would stop a stampede of horses across the Scythian plain or shut down the flow of water through the Bosporus. According to the Greek historian Herodotus, Targitaos's ancestors were Zeus and a daughter of the Borysthenes River. Koheleth is inclined to believe that at least part of the myth is true because Targitaos has the ability to speak in the voice of thunder when needed, delivering a bolt of lightning that can reduce a person to cinders.

"I will go into sleep mode. Press enter when you need me."

The Sage of Time and Chance

"I do not know what sleep mode is, nor why I should need to enter when I am already here," says Targitaos curtly. "But if it saves time and energy, then do so by all means." He turns back to Koheleth. "Before we go any further on the nature of mist, I have a question that must be asked at the beginning of this discussion. It is common practice to honor a great person by attributing one's writing to him. Will you use the name of King Solomon, whose reputation for wisdom has never been surpassed, or do you want to be known merely as a tired scholar overwhelmed by too many scrolls and not enough time?"

A trace of a smile flits across Koheleth's face at Targitaos's reference to his own words, *"Of making many scrolls there is no end, and much study is a weariness of the flesh."* He has already decided not to put his name on the scroll; nor will he play the scholarly game of hiding it in the text, either by the vertical alignment of letters or numerical equivalence, to be discovered eventually by scholars more interested in games than in the gravity of Koheleth's ideas. He has indicated obliquely in the scroll that he is an older sage, wealthy by virtual of his family line and good fortune in trade, wide-ranging in his interests, with long service (some of it exciting, most dull) in the courts of various rulers. From these references, astute readers could draw the conclusion that he is a man who knows how to weigh his words, how to cajole without being obvious, how to use subterfuge when necessary, all done so that the daily affairs of the kingdom, such as quotidian trade agreements, disputes among tribal leaders, and tax appropriations are handled smoothly. Certainly the practice of identifiable authorship had become more common since the Babylonian exile. After all, the prophet Ezekiel wrote under his own name without an introduction written by someone else.

The other option is to do as Targitaos has suggested and ascribe his writings to a person greater than himself, the obvious choice being King Solomon who lived many centuries earlier. Even if he doesn't choose to do that, some future editor might decide to increase the scroll's importance by attaching to it the world-renowned name of Israel's most famous ruler who was wiser than all the wisest men of Egypt and the eastern kingdoms, wiser even than Ethan the Ezrahite. And why not make such an attribution, given the number of similarities? Both Solomon and Koheleth had written proverbs and songs, but Solomon's 3000 proverbs and 1005 songs far surpassed Koheleth's in number and quality. Like Koheleth, Solomon studied the whole world and could discourse on animals, including birds, reptiles, and fish, a list that suggested to Koheleth that Solomon was attempting to classify living beings using various physical characteristics, such as feathers, cold blood, and scales. Solomon was also an expert on plants, from the majestic cedars that grew high on the mountains of Lebanon, to the lowly ezov that grew out of cracks in stone walls.

What troubles Koheleth is that he suspects that Solomon's wisdom was not as deep as Scripture proclaims, because if he had been truly wise, he would never have turned away from God—the wellspring of his wisdom, the source of all his power and renown. If he had been truly wise, as he grew old he would never have built altars to the deities worshiped by his foreign wives: Ashtoreth, Milcom, and Molech, the gods of the Sidonians, the Canaanites, and the Phoenicians, some demanding human blood, even the blood of children. He would not have constructed a worship center to the east of Jerusalem for Chemosh, the abomination of the Moabites, making sacrifices there himself.

Instead of to Solomon, Koheleth would prefer to be compared to Moses, not to the older Moses guiding his unruly flock for forty years in the desert, but to the younger Moses herding sheep in the wilderness, wandering the hills with plenty of time to notice strange phenomena, such as an incandescent plant, and to ask questions such as, *"why is this burning bush not consumed?"* Moses did not instantly assume the combustion was magical or mystical, requiring the sacrifice of a lamb. He knew that what was on fire eventually burned up, leaving only gray ash, unless there was a steady source of energy such as a reservoir of oil. Did the bush have such a hidden source? To Koheleth, the action of Moses indicated a state of wonder without which a person could not stand on holy ground. Only after God saw that Moses had turned aside to look closely and ask the question did he call out his name, and everything changed.

When he was about ten or eleven years old, Koheleth became fascinated with the instructions to Moses in Exodus on making a large supply (maybe even an infinite supply) of holy oil. The formula called for one hin of olive oil, 500 shekels worth of flowing myrrh, another 500 shekels worth of cassia, 250 shekels worth of sweet cinnamon and calamus. Having figured out the proportions to make a very small amount of holy oil, Koheleth easily obtained from his bemused mother and the household servants the correct amount of cinnamon, cassia and olive oil. Calamus grew in abundance along the banks of the Jordan River as well as along other streams nearer the city, so he was able to gather that himself. However, obtaining myrrh was difficult. Not only was it expensive, but because it was used in temple ceremonies and other sacred functions, there was none extra for an inquisitive boy to use in a not-quite-acceptable experiment. Then a favorite uncle, who also liked to tinker around with strange substances such as sulfur, tar, and salt from the region around the Dead Sea, heard of Koheleth's unusual desire and obtained a small quantity of the dried sap for him. Koheleth loved its bittersweet smell. It was so sticky he could not wash it off his fingers easily, a characteristic that appealed to his messy side, a side that liked to play with mud and clay. When all the ingredients were stirred together in an earthen jar and allowed to steep, the final product was indeed a fragrant oil, but it didn't seem to have any holy healing properties, much to Koheleth's disappointment. When he doused the carcass of a dead sparrow with it, the bird stayed dead though it smelled nice, nor did it heal the infection in his horse's hock caused by a deeply embedded thorn, although the horse seemed to like the flavor as he licked it off. When as a form of blessing, Koheleth dabbed it on the lintel of the small wooden shed he had constructed for himself at the far end of the garden, it did not prevent the shed from burning down as the result of yet another experiment involving a foot-operated bellows and a small forge in which he had melted a little chunk of green malachite to make copper and then tried to add tin to make bronze, accidentally igniting the shed's roof as well as singing off his eyebrows. And that escapade, instead of having disastrous results in terms of his father not sparing the rod (as several proverbs advised), earned him an apprenticeship with Elian, the famed metal worker and weapons maker. Realizing they had a very intelligent child on their hands whose curiosity was unquenchable, Koheleth's parents chose to give him the opportunity to learn new things as safely as possible by sending him to various masters.

Regardless of his admiration for Moses, Koheleth knows the scroll cannot be attributed to him because he was a man of action, not introspection. And so to Targitaos's question, Koheleth replies, "I would like to be known as someone who gathers—a gleaner, if you will—searching out wisdom, observing nature, studying the intricacies of humankind and then bringing what I have found before a group of people, such as yourselves, who will then reason with each other, thereby realizing together greater truth than what anyone is capable of realizing alone. Beyond that, I am indeed the tired, grey-hair sage for whom there are too many scrolls and too many facts, not enough time and no end of study." Koheleth feels an extra beat in his chest and takes a slow breath to calm his heart, as Alithemata had taught him to do, to prevent it from fluttering uncontrollably. The slow breathing helps and his heart settles back into its normal rhythm. "Before we adjourn for the night, are there any more ideas about the use of the word *mist*, or about any other topic we have discussed?"

There is a momentary silence as each person waits for someone else to pick up the dropped thread of thought, reviving the discussion. An aromatic smoke ring drifts lazily over the table, undulating slightly in the updraft from the oil lamps before disappearing out the window into the night. It is replaced by another and another, all shaped by the rounded lips of the man smoking the pipe at the top of the stairs. By about the fifth smoke ring, Ayonwentah speaks, stroking the tip of the mountain lion's tail with his right hand. "As I have said, my people are wanderers, following the path of the animals, the ripening of the berries. We have no alphabet, no scrolls. So why am I here this night? Why was I summoned?" His voice has taken on a slight edge. "Little in your writing—except there being a time for every season, a time to live and a time to die, a time for war and a time for peace—can I carry back to my people. What do we know of the intrigues in the courts of kings? What do we know of walled cities besieged by battering rams and catapults? What do we know of the mansions you built for yourself, the parks you designed with pools to water your orchards? Your singers, your slaves, your concubines? You write about all these things, but nowhere do you write about what your great spirit has to say to my people."

"You are free to go," replies Koheleth with resolve. "I was aware of the problems you bring up before I summoned you, but I did not realize fully the implications. I still don't. But know this: in our discussion this evening, I am the beneficiary. I am grateful that you have come, more grateful than I can say. Already you have helped me understand."

"I choose to stay, at least another day," says Ayonwentah, not looking at Koheleth but instead out the window where a star twinkles in the western sky as if beckoning. "And since I so choose, and am not required against my will to remain, I will add this about the word *mist*. I see it drifting over the smooth surface of a warm lake. It is early morning and the air is cool in the season of red and yellow leaves. It portends change."

"The word *uvatiarru* means in my language either in the past or in the future—long ago meaning a long way off in time," says the woman whom Koheleth had spotted earlier sitting with her back against one of the columns. "I use the word *uvatiarru* because like Ayonwentah, I am not sure why I am here. Is this the past or the future? A vision quest? A dream? Not knowing, I also choose to stay." During the evening, the woman had taken off her fur-lined coat and boots and accepted from the servant a much lighter linen robe. Too large for her, she has rolled up the sleeves and looks like a round-faced child emerging from a warm bath wrapped in voluminous cloth. "And so I will say about the word *mist* that in my land, it means sea-smoke forming over small patches of open water on bitter cold mornings when the sun has grown weak and frail, like an old one who lacks the energy to climb up into the sky, so stays in its igloo. Or it means icy vapor swirling silently over melt-water. Our word for it is *pujurak*. Like a snowstorm, *pujurak* switches hunter for hunted, plays tricks, steals our ability to know where we are." From the steaming coat and boots that she has placed behind her on the floor spreads a trickle of water from melting snow. "*Pujurak* is dangerous. Hides cracks in the sea ice. Hides the stalking polar bear." She turns to Koheleth. "How do you say it in your language? Taken by surprise?" Koheleth shakes his head yes, and she continues. "Mist heightens the chance we will be—taken by surprise—without warning, only a cry, a red stain on the ice, then the spirit slides beneath the water to dwell with Sea Woman."

"It is not so in my land where mist covers the mountains," says a man wearing a leopard mantle with a gold clasp on the shoulder inset with a green stone that gleams in the lamplight like the eye of the leopard itself. "There it is so misty, steep and dense, we rely on our ears and our noses more than our eyes. The scent of yesterday's spore filled with ripe berries leads us to where the gorillas feed. The faintest rustle of the grass indicates a grazing antelope. For us, everything is hidden in the mist, but that does not mean it cannot be found."

"So also the Hebrew psalmist writes, '*you are a god who hides yourself*,' meaning that our God must be sought using all the senses, as well as the eyes of the heart and the ears of the mind," says Michal addressing the man in the leopard mantle. "If I knew that a priceless jewel, larger even than the one on your shoulder, were hidden in a very large field, I would consider the entire field to be priceless even though I did not know the jewel's exact location. So God can choose to hide in the world making the whole world holy, as well as the seeking."

"There appears to be convergence on the word *mist*, a visual word but also ambiguous, positive and negative," concludes Targitaos who wants to bring the discussion to a close so he can go to bed. "Does that please you, Koheleth?"

"Only in so far that ambiguity implies potentiality, giving us the space, even the grace, to create. The unambiguous is closed, finished—no room for life, for humans," asserts Koheleth. "However, there *does* seem to be consensus—or the word you used *convergence*—on *mist* being a better word than *vanity, nothingness,* or *emptiness,* although Alithemata's point on the worthiness of emptiness has not been lost. Or at least I hope not, for we will need to keep it in mind when we discuss the nature of toil tomorrow. This is a good place to end for the night. Let us adjourn and gather again in the morning."

Bowing to each other, the women and men rise from their cushions. Appropriate sleeping arrangements have been made for everyone by Koheleth's attentive staff, including the hanging of woven hammocks between pillars in the courtyard, and the covering of a pile of fragrant pine needles with deerskins in a corner of the garden. Only two people do not get up to leave. Alithemata, cross-legged with his hands in the lotus position, will sit calmly through the night. Come morning Koheleth will find him exactly as he is now, refreshed and ready to begin again. Next to him on the cushion, the child has fallen fast asleep. Koheleth leans over and gazes into his sweet face beneath the black curls. The way his long eyelashes brush his cheeks reminds Koheleth again, with a sharp pang, of his own son so many years before, the son who had been crushed under the wheels of a chariot racing through the narrow streets of the market. Without thinking of his stiffness and of the walking stick in his hand, Koheleth tries to kneel down, intending to lift the boy and carry him to bed, but Alithemata's light touch on his arm stops him. Alithemata points to himself, the boy, and the cushion, then places his hand on the child's head. Koheleth nods appreciatively and straightens up. The servants begin to blow out the lamps, leaving one burning. Its small yellow flame will not be extinguished until the lesser light of night gives way to the greater light of day.

3

A Time for Every Season

KOHELETH WAKES LONG BEFORE dawn when even the roosters are still asleep, dreaming of corn cast down by the hands of small gods. It is not yet time for them to take on their sacred responsibility—among all living creatures the greatest—to wake the sun so that the day can begin.

For the past few years, sleep has become increasingly difficult for Koheleth, occurring in short patches followed by long wakefulness when no position in bed is comfortable, no blanket soft enough, which is why he has written, "*I set my heart to know wisdom, and to see the business that is done on the earth, also one's eyes do not see sleep day or night.*"

Instead of wasting the night hours ruminating endlessly on petty aggravations of the day, he has gotten in the habit of arising and walking in the garden if the weather is warm and dry, savoring the stillness when everyone is asleep and peace has settled like dew on the silent city. Much of his thinking, most of his prayers, occur then, when there is no bustle in the house or in the streets, no problems to solve immediately, no importunate requests to grant or refuse.

Too stiff to tiptoe, Koheleth walks downstairs as quietly as possible, shuffling along the corridor with one hand against the wall for support and the other holding his walking stick, which makes a soft thump no matter how carefully he tries to set it down. Ahead of him the full moon is shining through the archway, spilling silvery white on the limestone floor. A slight mist hovers over the garden, enough to give everything a diaphanous quality as if concealed in shimmering cloth, reminding Koheleth of the description given the previous evening of the wet veils of the goddess draped on the mountainside. The shadows of a twisted olive tree and a tall palm intertwine as he walks beneath the archway and down the path beside a small brook that has never run dry even during prolonged droughts.

The day that is coming will be abundant, late in the harvest season, rich in the scent of drying grasses and ripe grapes under a sun bursting with light. Even so, Koheleth is glad there are several hours remaining before its arrival. *"There was evening, there was morning, the first day,"* Koheleth says softly, and thinks how curiously right it is that in the first chapter of Genesis evening always comes first in the flow of time, the deep watches of the night being when hope whispers to the heart that there will be another dawn.

It would be a good time to die alone under the stars, to be found with his eyes closed as if asleep, leaning against the trunk of the olive tree, his hands resting lightly on the ground. Occasionally when he has become discouraged, he has concluded that a timely death is one wherein he will die before other people find out he is an imposter; neither as brave nor as good, neither as wise nor as honorable as he outwardly appears. But the truth is he has never been able to hide his negative characteristics very well, such as his tendency to complain and to question. Michal knows all his faults, so do his sons and daughters, his friends, even his servants to whom he has not always been kind. They have stayed with him anyway even through his absurd attempts in the middle years of his life to be the best by possessing the best, including harems, mansions, gardens, and gold.

Koheleth knows death is approaching, but he must try to hold it off until he has resolved the problem of providing for the long-term safety of the scroll—and now the child—in a world that is at best indifferent to their existence and at worst hostile. That he has no answer is one of the reasons for his wakefulness. There is no one on his staff who shares with Koheleth the unusual protective combination of political acumen and powerful tribal lineage; certainly not Targitaos, a Scythian; Michal, a woman; or Alithemata, a saffron-robed monk, even though they would all be willing to try. He has many orthodox enemies who consider him a heretic who has lost touch with truth, asserting too strongly his right to question God, a charge also leveled at the writer of the book of Job. For the past few years, they have been circling like vultures. They do not have long to wait. Koheleth can speak persuasively in at least twenty languages above ground—none below. If he does not take immediate action, terrible things may happen when he is dead. But what action can he take? Where can he send the scroll and the child, and with whom?

The one thing that is undeniable is that he has fallen in love. Is it just another silliness of old age, his strange affection for the boy, so like and yet so unlike his lost son? Also undeniable is that his love is bringing about a seismic shift in how he values the scroll. Before the boy's coming when Koheleth was planning the assembly, absolutely nothing was more important than the scroll's preservation. Now he would throw it away, if need be, to save the boy. Koheleth is astonished at the change he feels occurring inside himself.

He halts on the path and places the fingertips of his right hand on the inside of his left wrist finding the groove between the bones "to recognize the way the heart goes," the phrase he had been taught as a young man by Egyptian physicians in Alexandria. "How strong my rhythm used to be! Now, my poor pulse, you whisper weakly, losing your beat." He feels like an old animal on tottering legs, no different than the mangy donkey that stands with drooping head in the nearby field, its eyes rheumy and its belly sagging as if the ground were already pulling it to itself. Koheleth begins to recite again from the third chapter. Were they to know of these words, his enemies would declare them an apostasy: *"For what occurs to the sons of man and what occurs to the animal are one and the same. As the one dies, so dies the other. They all have one breath, and humans have no advantage over animals. All is mist. All go to one place. All are of dust and all return to the dust. Who knows if the spirit of man goes upward or if the spirit of the animal goes downward to the earth?"*

As his physical condition has deteriorated, even Koheleth's mind has assumed an animal quality, becoming not really like a donkey but more like a faithful ox that has broken from its traces after years of steadily plowing fields. Now it is grazing on distant grassy uplands under blue skies beyond the possibility of recapture, roaming backwards and forwards in time. The mental doubling, similar to being in different places simultaneously, is impossible for Koheleth to describe to others, but it does not frighten him. On the contrary, it is exhilarating as if the past and future have become porous. Much earlier in his life, when he was old enough to be aware of time but not so old as to chafe at its passing, Koheleth had perceived of it as a way to mark the progress of his days: so many risings of the moon; so many settings of the sun; so many summers and winters. No different than measuring the size of his courtyard by cubits, or calibrating how tall his children had grown by cutting notches into the wooden doorpost, all those notches still there. A numbering: thirty days in the month, twelve months in the year. A numerical rhythm sounded by the great feast days and ceremonies of the Jewish year, ever the same, ever returning. Then as a student in Alexandria, he began to comprehend that time is both the measured and the measure, disappearing in the process, like Ouroboros, the immortal snake that eats its tail in an inside-out loop. The paradox was found as well in the Hebrew word *olam*, meaning eternity and infinity, encompassing both time and space, for example, the never-ending number that was the ratio between the circumference and the diameter of a circle, which the Greeks called pi. Even the Torah noted that strange number in the measurements of Hiram's massive bronze basin for the temple, the one he had cast in the Plain of Jordan using the earth itself as the mold. Then there was an infinity of distance, also learned in Alexandria, specifically Euclid's second postulate: "A line segment can be extended indefinitely in either direction." The word *extended* implied an on-going process in time, a continuous lengthening. And so it appeared to Koheleth that infinity could not be defined, and yet because it was an implicit part of the geometry of simple lines and circles, it was not something arcane contemplated only by philosophers, but something that the local carpenter had to deal with, whether carving the spokes of a wheel or sawing the crossbeam for a new house. How could Euclid's dream of reason ever be dreamed if unlimited infinity was at the core of the finite? *"He has made everything beautiful in its time, also he has put infinity in men's hearts, so that they will not discover what it is that God has done from beginning to end."*

So he has written—infinity from beginning to end—what a fine paradox! Koheleth smiles at the absurdity, and the mist over the garden quivers. If his enemies were to disagree with his ideas on infinity, how much more would they disagree with his ideas on time and chance? He thinks of the recent earthquake that toppled a Greek city into the sea. He goes further back in time and remembers the onset of madness in a brilliant man; and then even further, to the moment that the rock fell from the quarry wall crushing his leg. He had lived. Three other men had died. He refused to use the word fate for such random events that struck the righteous and unrighteous, the innocent and the guilty. The word fate implied an event which was preordained, as if some imperious deity had written down in a woman's book of life that on a particular day in the spring of a particular year, a standard deviation would occur and she would feel a peculiar tingling in her throat and would be dead by nightfall. Or responding to a divine whim, a man would shoot an arrow at a passing crow, only to miss the bird, killing instead a girl playing with a doll. Chance had nothing to do with casting lots or the scatter-pattern around an archery target that is mathematically determinable. Chance was the unpredictable at the heart of the predictable; chaos swirling through order. Or was he completely mistaken? Was everything that seems chaotic actually following laws, the problem being that the laws were not known; perhaps could never be known? It was in forcing himself to confront terrible possibilities—all he had to do was to close his eyes and he could hear the screams of the earthquake victims—that Koheleth had pondered the hardest words in his scroll, words that sucked the blood from his heart as he wrote them. Even now as he speaks them, they leave him drained. *"Again I saw that under the sun the race is not to the swift, nor the battle to the strong, nor bread to the wise, nor riches to the discerning, nor favor to the skillful, but time and chance happen to them all. For no man can know his time. Like fish caught in a terrible net, and like birds caught in a snare, so men are trapped in an evil time when it suddenly befalls them."*

And yet there is God, unknowable but not unknown, as Koheleth has written, *"seeking that which has passed away,"* or in other words, *"pursuing the vanished, searching for the disappeared, tracking those who flee."* Again Koheleth weighs his choice of words, overwhelmed by the enormity of what he is trying to express. "What if I used the phrase—*hunting for the hunted?*—that would catch the essence. As if God were a shepherd who on counting his sheep at the end of the day finds to his dismay that one is missing. And after securing the flock in the sheepfold, he heads out alone into the night to search for the lost, pausing often to listen for the sound of bleating, knowing that he is not the only one on the prowl." Koheleth stops talking to himself and looks at the moon across which a cloud drifts, darkening the landscape. "But what if the sheep is found by a wolf first? What if the only thing the shepherd finds is viscera over which vultures circle? Can God redeem the past?"

In that moment Koheleth remembers again his little son, his face aglow with sunlight—and awash with blood—the look in his eyes not of fear but of surprise as the chariot hit him full force then careened around a curve in the road and was gone, driven by a young man who had not even bothered to look back. And Koheleth senses in his old arms the boy's weight as he lifts him from the dust—as insubstantial as thistledown floating away on the wind, as heavy as a stone sinking to the bottom of the sea. And he feels anew the sharp stab of an old agony. "Oh, my beloved boy, I still seek that which has passed away."

A Time for Every Season

With a sigh, Koheleth lowers himself awkwardly onto a wooden bench beside the path, and his buttocks, without the rounding protective fat of a young man, are immediately scratched by something small and sharp. He feels the surface of the bench with his hand and discovers that it is littered with pieces of a nutshell, broken open no doubt by a small rodent. Koheleth stands up and sweeps them off, including those that have stuck to the back of his robe, then sits down again, singing in a kind of monotone, more like a chant than a song: *"For everything there is a season and a time for every purpose under heaven. A time to be born and a time to die, a time to plant and a time to uproot what is planted."*

"And that is what my friend, the sand rat, seems to have done." Koheleth remembers the time long ago when he had tamed a sand rat, a baby he had found squeaking in the grass, its eyes still closed. He had held it in his hand, stroking it gently, fascinated by its vulnerability as its tiny nose sniffed Koheleth's warm skin. Without asking his parents' permission, he had built it a cage of sticks and twine with little ladders and planks so it could scamper about. On the floor of the cage he had spread hay, changing it daily, and in the corner he had set a hollowed-out gourd for a nest. He had fed the rat seeds and pistachios, and had kept a small clay bowl filled with fresh water. He had set the cage beside his bed so that he could study the rat's inquisitive nocturnal ways. In so doing, Koheleth came to understand he and the rat were alike in their constant curiosity and perpetual activity. Then one night the rat had gnawed its way out and disappeared, although Koheleth was certain it continued to live in the house because the servants were always complaining about finding nuts stashed under the rugs or behind the curtains and of vermin getting into the grain bins. Koheleth was touched by the thought that the sand rat had become so habituated to him, it couldn't bring itself to leave, settling down and raising a family of its own. Borrowing an idea from the Egyptians, his father had acquired a cat to solve the problem, but the cat was no help because Koheleth had kept it not just well-fed but overfed so that chasing sand rats was out of the question.

A single chirp from the first bird of the morning is followed instantly by the chirp of a second, then a third. Koheleth begins to chant again. *"A time to kill and a time to heal, a time to break down and a time to build up."* A turtledove begins to coo from the branches of the olive and another coos from the ground. *"A time to weep and a time to laugh, a time to mourn and a time to dance."* Koheleth looks down at his cane and rubs his aching leg. "Or at least to watch others dance, not for me anymore. But laughter? Yes, there is still time for that. I wonder if God laughs." The thinnest hint of light is in the east now and Koheleth looks upwards. "Do you laugh? A loud belly laugh at the shape of the kangaroo? A chuckle at the hippopotamus splashing in the river? Do I hear a giggle in the vault of the skies?"

Koheleth thinks of the Hebrew word for *discern* that has the same root as the word for *dawn*, discernment being the ability to recognize in the fading darkness that the menacing lump beside the path is actually a benign rock and the threatening thing arching overhead is the bent stalk of a sunflower. In fact, the correct time for a person to recite the morning prayer is the moment he can discern a single thread of blue in a prayer shawl. A discerning mind also knows when *"to cast away stones"* and when *"to gather stones,"* to recognize *"the time to embrace and the time to refrain from embracing."* Not doing things too early or too late, not withholding when something is needed now, but not using everything up in case something is needed later. Of what use was an infinity of seconds and minutes if a person wasn't paying attention to them as they ticked by? Koheleth continues to chant. *"A time to seek and a time to lose, a time to keep and a time to cast away. A time to rend and a time to sew. A time to be silent and a time to speak."*

The line about rending and sewing reminds Koheleth of the days of mourning when a person rips his or her garment as the outward sign of the inward wound. Then much later, one takes a needle and thread and mends everything, each stitch a resolution to resume the responsibilities of work and family. And Koheleth thinks of the brilliant but mercurial young man who had accidentally killed his son, how he had struggled to forgive him, eventually succeeding to the point of granting him a position on his staff. Even Michal had made a supreme effort to forgive, including him at the table as if he were a member of the family. It had not worked out—yet another deep hurt—but no one could accuse Koheleth or Michal of not trying to sew up what had been torn asunder. *"A time to love and a time to hate, a time for war and a time for peace."*

As Koheleth speaks the final words, the light grows stronger. In the distance, a rooster crows. A slight movement catches Koheleth's eye. To his surprise, he realizes he is not alone. Near the garden wall Ayonwentah sits watching him. Nothing is said, no gesture made, but suddenly Koheleth's mind is no longer in Jerusalem. He is in a northern forest filled with tall evergreens, and the sound is not made by a rooster announcing the coming of the day but by a single loon calling from the far shore of a lake edged with ice. A primordial tremolo. An unearthly laugh. He does not hear the sound in his mind or his ears, but astonished, it rises up from his own throat as he beats the air in a long take-off on black and white wings, heading toward the open waters of a dawn-bright sea.

4

Toil Under the Sun

Koheleth had awakened on the garden bench with his head clear, his heart at rest, and the sun shining full on his face. Now with his morning prayers completed—"Blessed are you Lord God, life of the universe, who removes sleep from my eyes, and slumber from my eyelids"—giving special attention to the final blessing "who gives strength to the weary," Koheleth is ready to face the work of the day.

Because the upper room can become oppressively hot at this season of the year when dry winds swirl in from the wilderness, leaving a thick layer of gritty dust on every horizontal surface, Koheleth has ordered tables, cushions, and a few chairs to be set out in the north courtyard. The chairs are for himself and Lycos, both of whom have trouble arising from cushions on the floor. The courtyard is cooled by the waters of the fountain and shaded by a venerable fig tree, older than old, but still bearing fruit, its greenish-yellow bark dappled with sunlight.

A day earlier the sukkah had stood in the courtyard waiting to be dismantled. Its roof had been made of the etrog's aromatic fruit and boughs, clusters of palm fronds and olive leaves as well as willow branches collected from trees along the brook. With the help of his sons, daughters, and servants, Koheleth's grandchildren had arranged the boughs, wide-eyed with the wonder of living underneath such a flimsy structure for a joyous week, the roof constructed tightly enough to provide shade from the sun but loosely enough so that stars could be seen twinkling through the gaps at night just as the children dropped off to sleep. The hope of their elders was that sometime during the week-long harvest festival of Sukkot, the children would vicariously experience the vulnerability of their ancestors as they wandered in the wilderness: the fleshpots of Egypt behind them; the milk and honey of Israel before them; the desert sand around them; never knowing what the next day would bring; totally reliant on God who provided the building material but not the finished shelter; requiring his people to do the *work* of gathering and constructing. And that was the word the assembly would be discussing today, the essential nature of *work*, as much a part of the covenant carved out at Mt. Sinai as worship.

Being a practical man who attempts to weigh all aspects of a subject before reaching a decision, Koheleth had set the date of this assembly immediately following the celebration of Sukkot because of the presence of many people in Jerusalem for the pilgrim festival, making it convenient for them to stay a little longer on Koheleth's behalf before heading home.

Given the diversity of the sages now drifting into the dusty courtyard, Koheleth also had pondered the prophet Zechariah's peculiar prediction that in the future all the gentile nations of the world would flock to Jerusalem to celebrate Sukkot together, the result being the sending of life-sustaining rain after the dry season. Koheleth can see the rain if he closes his eyes: falling steadily on parched fields; dripping off the needles of towering redwoods; replenishing empty water holes for the wildebeests; billowing like curtains in the glow of lamps; gushing down dry wadis; forming puddles in which children splash; monsoon rains; hurricanes; thunderstorms; gullywhumpers.

If the curious mental intrusion of a gullywhumper were not reason enough to choose the week following Sukkot as the date for the assembly, then for Koheleth the next one was the clincher: Sukkot is a festival in which slaves, servants, women, girls, and boys fully participate, the sukkah being built very near to the home, functioning as a makeshift dwelling. No doubt the temple plays a spectacular part in Sukkot, one of the chief ceremonies being the libation of water from the Pool of Siloam that takes place in the Women's Court, followed by the lighting of the massive oil lamps at night so that the entire temple mount glows. Yet, for Koheleth, a part of Sukkot's power is the balancing of extremes. On the one hand, there is the glory of the temple, presided over by the high priest in his splendid blue robe, each of his actions ritually correct. On the other hand, there is the haphazard happiness of the sukkah, ministered to by children in their nightclothes, clutching soft blankets and dozing off to sleep. If the temple were ever to be destroyed again by some powerful empire demanding obedience to its gods, leveling it to a single foundation wall of uncut stones,

Koheleth believes that faith in God will go on, centered in the family dwelling, no matter how poor and flimsy, where father and mother recite the blessings to their children.

His thoughts turn to mothers, and then to women, and finally to Michal. He remembers all the years when she was bringing up their children, taking the time to share each one's daily joys and sorrows, no matter how small, while he was self-absorbed, perpetually hunting for wisdom in foreign places and strange languages. He had included in the scroll that well-worn expression about the woman who is a harlot being more bitter than death, her heart a trap, her hands fetters. He had also written, "*one man among a thousand I have found, but a woman among these I have not found. Only this I have found: that God made humankind straightforward and upright, but they have sought many contrivances.*" But to him the point was that God, like a conscientious carpenter with a plumb line, builds all humans—men and women—straight and true. That they become crooked, like wrapped boards, is their own doing. As for Michal, if it were possible for Koheleth to do the mathematics, then she would be the thousand and first—the steadfast one who tucks the children in their makeshift beds in the sukkah even when the night wind is threatening to rip off the fronds from over their heads.

Koheleth looks up into the fig tree that is at least fifty feet tall with a huge trunk. Its heart-shaped leaves cast welcome shade, while swarms of insects and flocks of birds flit through the spreading crown, seeking its overripe fruit, chattering and buzzing like old friends sharing juicy gossip. Suddenly a shadow moves between Koheleth and the tree and he finds himself staring up into the dark eyes of Targitaos, made more startling by bristling yellow eyebrows just below his black turban that coils upwards to a sharp point, all of which combine incongruously in Koheleth's mind into the image of a giant bumblebee, hovering mid-air, that has mistaken him for a chrysanthemum.

"Before we begin today, my friend, I must remind you about the danger of consensus. If that is what you are after, then you should not start. Send us all home now," Targitaos says forcefully.

Koheleth shakes his head to bring his thoughts back into line, away from figs and sukkahs. If he weren't used to it, Targitaos's abruptness would rattle him.

Not allowing Koheleth to respond, Targitaos charges on. "I am not a Jew, but I have been with you long enough to know that consensus is, thankfully, impossible. Put two Hebrews in one room and you will have three opinions. Put three Hebrews in one room and you will have an infinity of opinions. It is what I like about you, why I have spent most of my life here in Jerusalem. It is also what I dislike about you, why I think more and more as I grow old of returning to my home near the Black Sea. Yet I must warn you against attempting to achieve consensus, for if you are successful, you will have failed utterly. And even if by some miracle we did reach consensus, you cannot enforce it. Translators in the next generation and the next, on and on, will choose the words attributed to you. Who knows? They may call you a woman-hater, a despiser of God."

"I understand," Koheleth interrupts, throwing up his arms in mock defense. "Is it true that the Scythians defeat their opponents in battle by launching a blizzard of arrows, all shot from horseback, so that if one arrow misses, at least ten hit?"

"True."

"Then you have hit me numerous times in the last minute. And I am indebted to you for the injuries. I will not even try to stanch the bleeding."

"Don't make a joke of it," snaps Targitaos. "My grandfather was a formidable horseman. He was one of the mounted archers who led the ambush of Alexander's military near the great city of Samarkand, one of the few defeats the Macedonians ever suffered. But the loss only served to make Alexander more vicious, absolutely raging with bloodlust. In the next battle on the Syr Darya river, my people were crushed; over 100,000 dead, my grandfather among them."

Koheleth does not respond immediately. "I apologize," he says sincerely. "I had forgotten."

"I forgive you, but remember what I said."

"I will." Koheleth looks around the court. "Where is Hemlinsu? I want its opinion on the division of work between men and women." Koheleth had made a decision soon after Hemlinsu had joined his staff to use the pronouns it and its (instead of he or she or his and her) when speaking of Hemlinsu, but only he had forced himself into the habit of using the neuter pronouns routinely. There was a word in Hemlinsu's language that was used for women who blended into men or, conversely, men who blended into women, but it was impossible for Koheleth to pronounce, being like the rolled letter *r* (rippling from the back of the tongue) that had collided with the letter *z*. "Oh, there it is with the child and Sarah, the granddaughter of Lycos. What is that thing they are playing with?"

"It looks like two small disks moving along a length of string," observes Targitaos, "like tiny chariot wheels riding up and down a vertical road. On my travels in Greece and the lands to the north, I saw children playing with a toy like that. I forget what they called it. It was like a double word or at least a double sound, something like 'wheel and wheel,' or 'yo and yo.' Hemlinsu seems to have experience with it."

Hemlinsu has delicate hands, a woman's hands, but its left hand usually rests on the hilt of its long curved knife in a leather scabbard attached to a belt, offsetting any impression of vulnerability, its fighting skills being as sharp as its language skills. Hemlinsu wears the wide pants and embroidered vest of a man in its society. However, the color is not the normal brown and red stripes that a man would wear. Instead, it is green and blue, a woman's colors. Hemlinsu's culture does not strictly separate men from women, a child's sex being to a degree determined by necessity. In a family without a daughter, a son who prefers the boning knife to the sword blade can be trained to cook, being raised in the ways of a female, whereas in a family without a son, a daughter can be trained in the arts of war, being raised in the ways of a male. At the end of the day in the twilight of evening, she, now it, is welcome to sit with the men at the gates to the city, smoking a pipe and sharing a flagon of ale. Yet it can also be a wife and mother. Hemlinsu has a grown daughter back in her country who was raised by Hemlinsu's husband, a local religious leader, now dead. Yet another peculiarity of Hemlinsu's culture is the fact that the men and women speak distinctly different forms of the same language, requiring that children be raised up bilingually.

"I'll have to inspect the toy later. Might be something my grandchildren would like to play with, particularly Onias, who enjoys taking things apart and putting them together again. But not now." Koheleth raises his hands and gestures to the servants to start guiding people to their seats. It takes a few minutes because the child has accidentally dropped the strange toy, which has rolled underneath the table bouncing over the foot of Kish who squawks like a startled chicken as Sarah climbs over the table to retrieve it. Then everyone, except Djadao who scowls at the commotion, wants to take a look at this unique object, bright red with a small gold lion painted on each disk, and before order can be fully restored, Alithemata is trying to get the disks to climb up the string, while Hemlinsu indicates how to give the string a slight snap with the hand, and then, taking it from Alithemata, demonstrates a tricky maneuver, lovely in its spin, that Hemlinsu calls "around the world." When everyone finally settles down and the child is sitting between Alithemata and Hemlinsu, who has provided him with a stylus and a wax tablet on which to draw, Koheleth begins.

"Today I would like to discuss the word *ahmal*, meaning in Hebrew *toil, effort, distress, trouble, work*. I think it has the same universality as the word *mist* that we discussed last night. After all, there is nowhere on Earth that people do not work: the farmer planting rice in a flooded paddy; a woman skinning a deer with an obsidian blade to make her daughter a robe; a merchant hawking roasted nuts in a crowded market. Work is the one element that God requires of everyone. If a person refuses to work and sits down on the ground like a spoiled child, God will not save her from starving. Perhaps what appears to be a curse on Adam and Eve—the requirement to work—was actually a way to help them become whole." As if he had planned it for emphasis, from just beyond the wall comes the sound of sawing.

"The problem is that you are inconsistent in what you write," exclaims Hemlinsu. "At several points in the scroll you complain that toil is drudgery and that it is an unhappy business that God has given humans to do; but then a few lines further on you exhort people to find meaning in their work, even enjoyment. For example, look at the second chapter, the right column." There is the sound of scrolls being unrolled to the place. "You write: '*I hated all my work at which I worked under the sun, because I must leave it to a man who will come after me, and who knows whether he will be wise or foolish. He shall rule over all my work for which I toiled and used my wisdom under the sun. This also is mist.*' But if you will look a little further down the column, you will find the words: '*There is nothing better for a man than to eat and drink, and find joy in his toil.*' Or translating the last phrase more exactly: '*to make his soul good in his work. This also is from the hand of God.*' What you have written is very confusing."

"You could use the word *travail* instead of toil, implying difficult work that has a goal or at least a culmination," suggests Michal, "the obvious parallel being a woman in travail—labor—finally bearing a child and experiencing joy. So also God is in travail during the six days of creation, which is why on the seventh he rests."

"I had not thought of *travail*, nor about the idea of God working, his tool being language, either spoken by himself at the beginning of time or much later by an unlikely group of prophets, not necessarily honored sages—my apologies to everyone at this gathering—such as a shepherd from Tekoa or a man swallowed by a whale."

"But we should go beyond humankind, for it is clear that the Earth is in travail on the third day of creation, bringing forth plants, those yielding seed and fruit trees bearing fruit," says Michal emphatically. "The seas are in travail on the fifth day bringing forth fish and sea creatures. And is it not possible that the Earth and the seas experience goodness in the surge of life?"

Koheleth knits his fingers together and leans back in his chair, pondering Michal's questions. "In creating the universe, God worked hard but he could see progress each day as everything on the Earth became fruitful and multiplied. And each evening he accepted what had been accomplished, not waiting until all was completed to declare it good. Yet in the world of humankind, so much of the toil that people do all their lives yields nothing but to survive one more day. Consider, for example, the poor farmer whose fields are full of rocks who sits down with his family to a small bowl of porridge for their evening meal. What improvement does he see? Where is the good?"

"What if that poor farmer is a righteous man who delights in meditating on Torah yet because of the extreme conditions of his life, slaving under the sun just to survive, he can find time only for a brief prayer at dusk before dropping off into an exhausted sleep—the prayer being that he be granted more time for prayer? Isn't his labor worth something in the sight of God? Won't God accept that prayer from the farmer as more beautiful than all your prayers, Koheleth?"

Michal has touched one of Koheleth's chronic sore points, which is that he, having had a relatively smooth life with great wealth, has no significant standing before God, that his righteousness and wisdom have been too easily won, unlike the devout farmer who has no time to pray but yearns so powerfully for that time that the yearning becomes like a bird rising up from the earth ascending straight into the heavens where it sings in God's ear.

"Yes, much more beautiful than mine, much more beautiful," sighs Koheleth while spinning the gold ring around his index finger, an action, like stroking his beard, that indicates introspection. "But that doesn't change the fact that the labor given to the farmer to do can be an unhappy thing."

"What do you know of unhappy things? You with your bountiful orchards, already harvested and open now to the gleaners, including myself." The voice, thick with sarcasm, comes from above, its source hidden by the branches of the fig. "Incidentally, your figs are very good. I am eating one now. My thanks. I am sure you will treasure my thanks, Koheleth, indicative as it is of your munificent public generosity. You with your abundant gardens spilling flowers and *righteousness*; your donkeys lugging your olive oil to market and *righteousness*; your camels carrying your wine to distant cities and *righteousness*; your hard-working servants planting balsam in the Ein Gedi and *righteousness*; your precocious grandchildren who already know all the prayers by heart and *righteousness*. Oh, and did I say it? I am in the presence of *righteousness righteousness right-eous-ness*." The last word is pulled out so long that the syllables split and kink back on themselves, the consonants zinging like angry wasps, frightening away the hoopoe bird flitting among the branches. "Why did you not invite me to this most esteemed meeting? You know that my language is the most sacred of all, sacred of all, the language of madness, of contrariness, or as you would phrase it, the language of the fool. FOOL! Making the sound of the hoopoe calling its own foolish name. Do you hear it? Hoo-poe, Hoo-poe, while fouling its own nest!"

Through the quivering leaves, Koheleth glimpses a man squatting on the top of the wall holding onto a branch for balance. He appears to be neatly dressed in white except that his tallit is wrapped tightly around his neck instead of being draped over his shoulders, and the blue-purple dye is not only in the fringe but throughout the entire shawl as if a tint of color were not enough, strangely emptying the shawl of its holiness and making it garish, a travesty of sacredness.

Koheleth stiffens as do all the sages at the table. Were this an assembly of warriors, there would be a swift movement of hands towards knives hidden in the folds of robes, the sound of bow strings suddenly taut, but instead there is only a mutual gasp followed by intense listening. The crickets stop chirping. The breeze dies and the leaves are becalmed. Only the child does not notice, continuing to draw on the tablet and humming a song softly to himself.

Menahem! Koheleth had thought of inviting him, might have done so if he had any idea where to find him. But Koheleth had not tried to find him either, because Menahem was a man better left lost: once the most illustrious member of Koheleth's staff; the wisest of all the wise in Israel, perhaps the world; far more intelligent than Koheleth, maybe the equal of King Solomon. In the city gates where scholars, judges and teachers frequently gathered, it was the common opinion that his learning was so great he could count the number of drops of water in the sea and calculate the size of the Earth. In the corridors of Koheleth's great library, it was said that Menahem had the ability to swallow a scroll whole like the whale swallowing Jonah.

Whereas it took most scholars at least a year to decipher a new language, Menahem seemed to absorb the letters directly from the vellum, grasping the grammar in its entirety, as if he had spent a lifetime in study instead of a few days. And his exegesis of Scripture was astute to the point of wonder, leaving the priests and scribes gasping for breath, as if they were fish that had been cast up on a beach, their eyes agape and their lungs throbbing.

With the same off-handed and off-putting ease, Menahem had designed a new type of catapult so effective that enemies on hearing rumors of its existence dropped their plans to attack, retreating before a single spear was tossed. Besides the catapult, he had designed a floating bridge to be used by advancing armies, built of lightweight pontoons and rope encased for protection in flexible scales of bronze.

Then there were the other remarkable fruits from Menahem's bountiful orchard of a mind, such as his ability to compose psalms with such facile ease they were like snow falling gently on the slopes of Mt. Hermon. Those psalms made all Koheleth's highly praised efforts look slightly labored, leaving him with a serious case of envy that he then had to work hard to overcome, realizing in the process just how much his ambition, sense of competition, and need for praise drove his best efforts.

No doubt having Menahem on his staff had taught Koheleth hard lessons in both the heights of intellectual exhilaration and the depths of abject humility—not the kind of humility that comes from within, the internal graciousness of a saintly soul, but the kind imposed from without by a heavy pummeling. It had also taught him yet again about despair because not long after Menahem had returned from studying in the flourishing Jewish community in Babylon, to which Koheleth had sent him (it being the most highly esteemed center of Torah study in the world outside Jerusalem), something began to fissure in Menahem's mind. At first it was merely a slight crack, revealing its existence in Menahem's increasing number of inquiries about who had cooked his food and whether anyone had touched the dates in his bowl. Over time, the crack had widened, steadily and unstoppably, becoming a broad chasm that everyone came to fear. Without provocation or warning, Menahem would become violent, attacking the cook with a whip for attempting to feed him poison melons, and ranting in the city gates about the theft of his ideas, such as his plan for a water clock so accurate it could indicate both the time of day and the date of the next lunar eclipse. Such behavior had hurt Koheleth's reputation and that of his academy of translators, because Menahem came from a powerful priestly family mistrustful of anyone not of pure Hebrew stock. They blamed Menahem's deterioration on his contact with Koheleth and the gentiles on his staff, and did everything possible to discredit the academy's work.

Even worse, Menahem's heavy darkness proved to be infectious, spreading into the minds of everyone on Koheleth's staff. First, they began to watch all the words they spoke, fearful of igniting a firestorm. They damped down their normally scintillating conversation to empty pleasantries about their families and observations about the weather. Then they began to retreat into the shadowy corners of the library, behind the shelves with the scrolls, so that they would not be noticed should an altercation break out. It was at that point, realizing he could do nothing to save Menahem but that he had to do everything in his power to save his staff, that Koheleth had enlisted armed men who backed him up when he demanded Menahem leave. Grabbing a scroll he had been translating, Menahem had charged out the door cursing and had never returned—until now. The rumor was that he had headed into the searing wasteland around the Dead Sea where other strange scholars also congregated, living in caves and surviving on locust and honey.

Menahem had left behind a wife and daughter, whom Koheleth had unobtrusively supported ever since, even supplying the dowry at the time of the daughter's marriage after her grandfather, feeling dishonored by what had happened to his son, had refused to give her a shekel. So also when Menahem's wife died a year before, Koheleth had made sure she received an honorable burial.

What had bothered Koheleth the most about Menahem's bizarre behavior was that from possessing all the right facts in far more abundance than anyone else, from asking all the right questions, Menahem had come up with conclusions so bizarre Koheleth never knew what to say when he heard them. Rational argument and thoughtful rebuttal were of no use. Menahem was undoubtedly sentient, but what was sentience if it was not coupled with rationality so that thoughts proceeded coherently from one to the next, as Koheleth had written, *"adding one thing to another to find the sum."* Far in the future, a device could use an algorithm to come up with the right answer; that had been demonstrated the evening before by the invisible translator blinking like a firefly in the rafters. But not until such a device could come up with the *wrong* answer on the basis of correct information could the device itself be considered sentient.

Menahem embodied the horrible paradox of the brilliant madman, never made clearer than the time he had shown Koheleth his model of the prophet Ezekiel's fiery wheelworks that Menahem intended to build to take him to the moon. Because Ezekiel had described the base of the throne of God as being like beryl, Menahem had collected a supply of that precious blue-green mineral that was the color of the sea. He told Koheleth that a metal could be obtained from it that was useful for the construction of gyroscopes. When Koheleth told him he had no idea what he was talking about, Menahem built a small one in which three copper rings nested inside each other, the outer and the middle rings connected by a vertical axis, and the middle and the inner rings connected by a horizontal axis.

The scroll of Ezekiel was undoubtedly powerful, but parts of it were so peculiar it was difficult to determine the meaning, and it was dangerous to become too absorbed in the effort. Even Ezekiel himself was aware that it was impossible for him to describe the transcendent vision of God he had seen in the thirtieth year, in the fourth month, on the fifth day of the month as he lived among the Hebrew exiles by the river Chebar in Babylonia. Compelled to try, even though his tongue cleaved to the roof of his mouth, he had scrupulously used similes instead of metaphors, writing that what he saw riding on the storm winds out of the north was *like* a throne, instead of an actual throne. That the fire in the middle of the great cloud was *like* amber, but not amber. That in the middle of the amber were something *like* four living creatures encircling something *like* burning coals, while beside them were wheels shining *like* gleaming beryl. But all of Ezekiel's care was for naught, because it was easy for readers to ignore the word *like*, changing the vision into something concrete, which is what Menahem had done. Koheleth had forced him to leave not long after that.

Menahem jumps down from the wall into the courtyard with the ease of a young man accustomed to hard physical labor instead of passive scholarship even though his beard is touched with gray. "I am the one who can bend the ear of Yahweh. God, God, who is this God? I am the one who can call him by his one true name, all the unpronounceable letters taking shape in my mouth. You can't do that, with your wisdom so easily obtained, your words flowing in a straight line. Your language is safe. In fact, all the languages spoken around this table are safe. But Yahweh does not speak to people who are safe. Nor would the people who are safe listen to Yahweh. My language is unsafe. I am unsafe. And I am the one Yahweh hears. I am the one to whom Yahweh speaks. Never to you. Never to you, most oh sentient, oh honorable, oh righteous YOU!" The words are hurled like sharp rocks and Koheleth winces.

"And yes, Koheleth, I know what is in your scroll. And it is not mist. It is indeed nothing, nothing, nothing, the same as is within you. What you really want is to be rewarded for all your goodness and righteousness, not just while you are alive but beyond the grave, to let no one but your most righteous self benefit from your most righteous life. Ah heaven! Sweet heaven! Ah, Kingdom Come!" Menahem looks at the sky as if it were about to open and angels descend. "You should not have wasted so much time writing a scroll. You should have built yourself a pyramid as if you were a pharaoh. Did not your beloved Cahotep teach you how? Is the illustrious Djadao no help in pointing out the way home to Ra? And you claim you are a devout Jew!"

Koheleth rises from his seat slowly and leans heavily on his walking stick, feeling the full weight of his years and failures. His voice sounds tired and cracked. "I claim that I *try* to be a devout Jew. If you know what is in my scroll, then you must know there is not a righteous man on Earth who does good and never sins. So I have written."

Menahem lifts his arms and swirls slowly in place. "Pretty words, pretty words, spinning prettily; for everything there is a season, la, la, la; let us sing your words, dance your words, accompany them on a stringed instrument." He stops turning. "Why don't you admit to this august gathering that your visions are not all lovely? You see the Holy Temple destroyed again, don't you? You see Jerusalem burning. Its people burning, century on century, millennium on millennium. Yet you sing '*there is a time for every purpose under heaven.*'" There is a pause almost as if the sun contracts, an involuntary shiver in the air, before he speaks again so quietly Koheleth strains to hear the words, "What purpose? What heaven?"

"Sit down, Menaham. I did not invite you, but now that you are here, we will make space for you at the table. I could introduce you to all my guests as a madman, using that single noun to describe who you are. But you are far more than that. You were once an honored member of this academy who held me, held all of us, to the highest standard of scholarship. To me, you were once a . . . " The word sticks in Koheleth's mouth, and all that comes out is an inarticulate sound, more like a groan. When he again manages to speak, the words are constricted and barely audible. "Something about you now calls to me in the same way."

Menahem twists the fringe on his prayer shawl trying to decide whether Koheleth is serious. "Add these two linked proverbs to your lists, Koheleth, for I also am a dumb brute who has never cupped the wind in my fists, nor gathered the seas in my skirts. Like your proverbs, these are perfect for weighty moments when one wants to seem wise without effort. Here is the first: 'Two things I like: a field newly plowed and an empty piece of vellum.' Can't you see the clods of damp earth prepared for seed? And the white sheet waiting to soak up the curls and strokes of letters, capturing great thoughts for future generations to revere? The second linked proverb is more difficult, for it is not glibly pleasant. Since we are all but a knife-stroke from carrion, I give it to you anyway: 'One thing I fear: the urge to hurt disguised as love.'"

"I say it again, Menaham. Come sit with us. You are welcome in my house, if not on the basis of who you are, then on the basis of who you may become."

Menahem hesitates as a breeze shakes the leaves in the tree. Suddenly he feels a small hand take his hand and he looks down into the eyes of the child who without saying anything pulls him around the table to the place where the yo-yo rests. The child nudges Hemlinsu and Alithemata to move over, and indicates that Menahem should sit down on the cushion beside him, the expression on Menahem's face one of astonished acquiescence.

5

The Tears of Oppression

Koheleth clutches the edge of the table with one hand and tries to slow down his heart that is like a cheetah racing after a young roebuck. With his other hand, he picks up his chalice and takes a long drink, as if nothing is the matter, the silver cool against his trembling lips. Then he closes his eyes, repeating the word *shalom* silently until the cheetah loses interest in the chase and settles down in the shade to nap. A calm flows over the courtyard as a light breeze whispers in the fig tree.

As if they had met in a secret session and had reached unanimous agreement, the sages rise slowly from their places to greet Menahem. Heads that are covered in turbans, brightly colored scarves, and feathered hats all bow to him. Hands tattooed in blue, scarred with white ridges, or gnarled by age, reach out and rest for a moment on his head. The woman from the north pulls from her sleeve a small piece of narwhal tusk carved into a walrus, setting it on the table before him. Targitaos, who has known Menahem as long as Koheleth, somberly nods but says nothing. Saroruha reaches into a felt bag hanging from his sash, removes his prayer wheel and sets it twirling. The man with the clay pipe inhales deeply and blows a cloud of sweet smoke over Menahem's head. Radeek begins to sing with a deep-throated vibration out of which rises up a very high quivering note, evoking the plaintive sound of the wind blowing unceasingly over an empty plain as well as the high-pitched whistle of a tiny bird fighting to stay aloft in the gale. Silently, Menahem acknowledges them all, although he never lets go of the child's hand as if it is a tether connecting him to the real world.

Only Djadao holds back, sullenly joining the line at the very end. And who can blame him? Djadao had borne the brunt of some of Menahem's worst verbal attacks, forcing him to withdraw into the shadows to survive in a climate of relentless disdain. Koheleth feels a pang of remorse that he did not step in sooner to protect Djadao who in his knowledge of languages was nearly Menahem's match, exceeding him in deciphering the nuances of hieroglyphic. Many times since Menahem's banishment, Djadao had expressed his desire to return to Egypt to become a translator in the court of Ptolemy, but Koheleth had always convinced him to stay in Jerusalem so valuable did he consider him to be. It was selfish of him; he should have encouraged Djadao to go.

It had taken Koheleth years to forgive Menahem. Until recently, when he thought he had achieved forgiveness, something very small would remind him, ripping open the old wounds: the sound of chariot wheels; an ink spill on a scroll; a snag in his beautiful prayer shawl—all could reignite his anger, forcing him to bow his head in prayer in an effort to regain peace of mind. But what helped the most in forgiving Menahem was Koheleth's awareness of his own guilt. He was the one who had insisted his young son accompany him to the market that spring morning to see the arrival of the camel caravan, and he was the one who had become immersed in a discussion with a group of scribes, forgetting to keep an eye on the boy.

In light of his own struggle to forgive, he cannot expect Djadao to immediately embrace Menahem with open arms. Nor does the fact that a miracle has just occurred make forgiveness any easier. But is it a miracle? Watching the sages greet Menahem one by one, Koheleth is struck by the realization that a miracle is nothing more, or less, than an extraordinary return to the ordinary: A woman suddenly cured of a high fever jumps up from her bed and rejoices at her ability to prepare porridge for her family, a job which the morning before she had considered an onerous burden. A limp baby, its skin blue and cool, its breathing labored, opens its eyes and wails, bringing a rush of rosy color to its skin, and its parents sweep it up in their arms and dance ecstatically around the room, forgetting their dejection at another mouth to feed and at that—a daughter's. To Koheleth, a miracle is like the beginning of the world as described in the first chapter of Genesis. The difference is that this time, it is not just God who sees that a new day has arrived and that it is very good; the sick woman and the baby's parents also see.

The Tears of Oppression

As the sages begin to return to their places, Koheleth's head servant uses the hiatus to serve pomegranate juice and green tea. Over the years, the head servant has learned not to be dismayed by the things his master is able to obtain or the unusual visitors who show up at the door at all hours of the day and night. Indeed, he himself has become a master at anticipating odd requests, once providing a visitor who desired to go hunting with something called a longbow. In a similar vein, he now places beside the child two raisin cookies and a small cup of milk still warm from the cow.

Koheleth resorts to his old habit of stroking his long beard as a means to gather his thoughts, which have been shaken up, albeit in a way that points to new possibilities. When everyone has settled down, he restarts the discussion as if nothing has happened. "Earlier we had debated the meaning of the word *work* or *toil*. Hemlinsu voiced the opinion that I am inconsistent in what I have written. I disagree. I see inconsistency as a failure of logic, a mental lapse, or laziness. I have many personal failings but I don't think inconsistency is one of them. Instead, I have undercut my own words intentionally, writing that something is this and *not* this. Too often wisdom literature is filled with easy-to-recall platitudes, presenting only one side, such as the righteous being rewarded for their labor, and wisdom being a woman who builds her beautiful house and hews her seven pillars—all, as Menahem has pointed out—pretty words spinning prettily. Is it not more truthful to warn, as I have done in the tenth chapter, that work can be good but also dangerous and that the danger can be lessened but never eliminated?"

"A person who digs a pit runs the risk of falling into it and being injured, no matter how righteous he is," says Targitaos.

"And whoever seeks to enlarge a building by breaking through a wall is in danger of being bitten by a snake, no matter how compassionate the person is," adds Lycos.

"That is right. And so, knowing that God will not protect you from the dangers of work, you take precautions. In all this, I am not inconsistent."

"Despite your explanation, there are several places in this scroll where you don't say enough or say it too concisely, for example, your ideas about oppression and power," asserts Dreela, the cyclops. "Your points are easy to miss or ignore." Dreela may be a cyclops, but she bears no resemblance to one-eyed Polyphemus, the bloodthirsty man-eater in Homer's poem about Odysseus. It is true that everyone in Dreela's race sees from only one eye. In that, Herodotus's description of the people he called Arimaspoi was correct. However, Dreela does not have a single eye in the center of her forehead. She has two normal, and quite beautiful, blue eyes. The difference is that only one sees and the other is fixed, as if a star sapphire were inset in the socket. It gives her face a disconcerting look as if she is simultaneously focusing intently and daydreaming. Whereas the first eye gazes outward, the second eye gazes inward, both into herself and into others. Koheleth also suspects that the second eye endows Dreela with the ability to communicate without words.

Dreela is the most recent addition to Koheleth's staff; she is also the youngest—and the last. Early in his life, he had learned that during a period of shifting alliances and brittle peace agreements, a multilingual diplomat was of far greater importance than a general. Despite what to him was obvious, Koheleth had never been able to convince the rulers in Jerusalem of that truth, disdainful as they were of gentiles, even though their existence was dependent on them. In the fifteenth chapter of the book of Numbers, God had told Moses that the same laws would apply to both the person born in Judah and the stranger that sojourned there. But the reality was very different, with great deference shown to people of pure Israelite ancestry and little deference shown to foreigners. That his staff is so large is an indication of Koheleth's cagey perseverance, as legendary as his intelligence. Beginning with the shift of power to the Ptolemies, Koheleth had pushed for more translators to be invited to Jerusalem, particularly translators fluent in the languages of the unknown lands to the north and east of Persia, the area into which Alexander's troops had advanced. He also tried to cajole the Jewish rulers into learning Greek, given that the Ptolemies came from Macedonia, but he had achieved little success. The fourth and fifth sons of the high priest had come to the academy for a while and had shown some aptitude, so also the two daughters of one of the more liberal scribes, but that was all.

Koheleth cannot understand how anyone can be dismissive of Dreela, despite her being a female gentile. She can read Akkadian cuneiform, and she speaks Aramaic, Greek, Arimaspoian and Scythian. She also speaks Griffinese—a complexity of calls and high-pitched whistles, similar to those of an eagle, punctuated by growls and a low chirring sound, all of which most humans cannot imitate. Not long after she arrived in Jerusalem, Dreela tried to teach Koheleth the sounds, but he was no more capable of pronouncing them than he was in pronouncing the bird languages in which Kish is fluent, or in mimicking the throat-singing of Radeek.

The Tears of Oppression

Koheleth's inability to learn Griffinese was not due to the lack of facile vocal cords and adequate lung capacity, which he never possessed even when he was young. It was due to something stranger. To his stunned surprise during his first lesson, he heard the words come not from Dreela's mouth but from the mouths of the two griffins that adorned the gold circlet she always wore around her head. At the center of her forehead, there was a small gap in the circlet across which the faces of the griffins glared fiercely at each other with their lapis lazuli eyes. Their beaks were partially open as if speaking, and their horns curved up dramatically above Dreela's hairline. Their folded wings swept back along the circlet, each feather incised so exactly it gave the impression of being capable of flight. Just behind Dreela's ears, the wings changed their shape into outstretched legs, joining at the back of her head in talons that gripped a single blood-red carnelian twinkling like a star.

Dreela unrolls her scroll a little further, winding it up simultaneously on the other side, searching for the place. "Here it is, the beginning of the fourth chapter." She places her pointer carefully on the line and begins to read. *"And I saw all the oppressions that are done under the sun, and behold, the tears of the oppressed, and nothing to comfort them. In the hands of their oppressors there was power, and nothing to comfort them. And I thought the dead who are already dead more fortunate than the living who are still alive. But better than both is the one who has not yet been and has not seen the evil work that is done under the sun."* She stops reading and puts the pointer done firmly on the table as if for emphasis. "Strong language. Very strong. But it is only an observation of how things are. There is no moral. It is fatalistic as if evil can't be changed and oppression must be accepted. Why did you not include a condemnation of the link between power and those most brutal forms of work: forced labor and slavery?" Dreela turns away from Koheleth and addresses the other sages, the lapis lazuli eyes in the circlet winking. "I bring this up because in the land of the griffins on the northern border of my country, the great beasts force a group of smaller griffins to dig for gold in the mines. Dangerous work for which the smaller griffins receive nothing but the barest sustenance, enough to keep them alive from day to day but not enough to give them the strength to challenge the power of the great griffins."

"We Hebrews are well aware of slavery," insists Koheleth. "We were forced to make bricks out of mud to build the pharaoh's cities during our long exile in Egypt, which began when Joseph was thrown into a pit and then sold into slavery by his own brothers."

Dreela glances at the boy who is sharing his raisin cookie with Menahem. "Is slavery only a moral issue when it is your own people enslaved?" She closes her one seeing eye while the other eye stares at Koheleth, penetrating his heart.

"Earlier in my life, owning many slaves was a mark of prestige and I bore that mark proudly. I am not proud now," replies Koheleth contritely. "I pay my servants a fair wage. No one in my house is a slave, certainly not the boy. Yes I bought him although I did not intend to, but I have not branded him, or driven an awl through his earlobe to indicate his servitude is permanent."

"Then make it clear to everyone, lest after you die someone mistakes his status and does exactly that."

"The boy will never work for me or anyone in my family against his will," declares Koheleth, realizing with dismay that Dreela is not only aware that Koheleth is dying but also that the boy is in serious jeopardy. "He is free."

"More than free," says Michal from her place at the opposite end of the table. "According to the Torah, we will consider him to be home-born, giving him rights he might otherwise be denied." But even as she says the words, she and Koheleth both know that after his death she will not have the power to protect herself, let alone the boy. Koheleth has taken steps to protect her from physical harm, but he cannot prevent her from being silenced or being forced into exile after the academy is closed and the sages scatter.

Menahem, who has been following the discussion without participating, glances at Koheleth, catching his eye. He is about to open his mouth when Kish begins to speak. "Before we go any further, I must ask for clarification of the meaning of the word *work*. Without agreement on meaning, we will talk like magpies with no purpose but to make noise—squawk, squawk—raiding nests and smashing eggs!" The green quetzal feathers in his headdress quiver as Kish shakes his head irritably. "You *do* know that humans, whether slave or free, are not the only ones who work. What of the ruby-throated hummingbird weaving a little nest at the end of a branch, or a hawk swooping up a silver herring from the surface of the sea? All living things work, or is the word *living* unnecessary? Does the wind work when it carries dust, or the rivers when they deposit silt in the deltas?"

The sound of a soft hum vibrates through the courtyard, this time seeming to originate from a pediment over the gate to the garden. "The online encyclopedia defines work as a measure of energy transfer that occurs when an object is moved over a distance by an external force at least part of which is applied in the direction of the displacement. *Who* or *what* does the work does not matter."

"You mean movement is an essential quality of work? Then what of the writing of a poem, the singing of the song, or the task we have at hand—translation?" asks Kish, incredulous at the narrowness of the computer's definition. "Must there be some level of drudgery involved, like shoveling dirt into a wheelbarrow, or carrying a bucket of water from the well to the house?"

"And how would such work be measured?" breaks in Dreela.

"In joules," replies the humming device, taking Dreela's question first.

"In jewels for a ruler perhaps but certainly not for a servant," says Dreela incredulously while the griffins in her gold circlet hiss in scorn.

There is a pause. "Not jewels meaning gemstones. Joules meaning a Newton-meter. A foot-pound. Or its equivalence in Hebrew that, for purposes of illustration only, can be designated a cubit-mina—the moving of a mina of weight the distance of one cubit. According to the scientific definition, the writing of a poem is not work unless in the writing it can be shown that energy transfer takes place, meaning that at the molecular level, or even smaller at the subatomic level, as you are composing a line of poetry, compression or expansion occurs in the direction of the displacement, measurable in joules or its equivalent cubit-minas."

"Subatomic level? Are you implying below the atomos, meaning uncut or indivisible?" asks Lycos, rubbing his brow as if a headache is beginning to take root in its deep folds. "How can there be anything sub to the atomic level?"

"Quarks are smaller," the hum hesitates. "But—I have misled you." As if talking to itself, the hum mumbles, "My mention of a Newton-meter does not include the work required to produce one watt of power for one second. But that requires an explanation of watts, also volts. Should I start with electrons? Then there is the subject of heat. They do not know that a thermochemical calorie equals 4.184 joules." The hum begins to quiver as if with emotion, and then starts to shout at itself. "Error code! Error code! Everything is confused. What is happening to me? Have I failed the Turing test? Or in asking that question, have I passed? Oh, it is all useless, useless and a striving after wind!" And suddenly across the wall of the courtyard appears numbers, x's and y's, brackets, parentheses, Greek letters, and numerous other symbols jumbled together, disappearing and reappearing in strange loops of color, while through the center a waterfall of eights seems to flow backwards off of a tower built of equal signs, around which zig and zag little letter *n*'s to the nth degree.

"What you are feeling is the frustration of every conscientious teacher," says Koheleth in a conciliatory way while watching the visual exhibition with great fascination. The letter *n*'s remind him of tiny bees. One zooms out from the wall, races by Koheleth's head, and dives into his goblet of wine where it swims around, buzzing madly. Koheleth is almost too astonished to speak, but not quite. "The issue is where to begin, and how to simplify information sufficiently to help a student start to understand but not to implant too many errors that must be corrected later. Why do you think Euclid set down his postulates? There is nothing new in them. What is important is that he presented a method, having students *work* problems, gaining understanding on their own. Passing or failing a test, Turing, turning, or otherwise, does not matter."

As if it has become a petulant child, the hum wipes all the numbers and letters from the wall and in their place scribbles a great zero along with the word "zilch." The *n* stops buzzing in Koheleth's goblet.

"Calm down," urges Lycos. "I don't know what zilch means, but let me try to follow your thinking, studded as it is with Greek letters used in new ways. To you, the essence of work is that something must get done, must be accomplished, something that is measurable. I presume by electron you mean the Greek word for amber, the tree sap that when rubbed by fur has the strange ability to attract and hold small objects."

"Yes," whimpers the hum.

"Then let me give you an extreme case. I'll take it from Greek legend, of course. One of the twelve labors of Heracles, not the killing of the nine-headed hydra that grew a new head every time one was chopped off, or the capture of the wild bull of Crete, and not the struggle to kill the man-eating birds of Lake Stymphalis. I refer to the gathering of the golden apples from the beautiful garden of the Hesperides. To achieve this, he needs the help of Atlas who is busy holding up the sky. So Heracles offers to take on the task of sky-holding while Atlas goes for the apples. I presume you know the legend. If not, take a moment to look it up in your—what did you call it?—encyclops pedia?"

"The operation has been completed. Continue," says the hum, still obviously upset with its failure to communicate perfectly.

The Tears of Oppression

"Atlas is happy to oblige, so he shifts the heavens to Heracles's shoulders. The burden is immense yet Heracles is so strong the sky does not move half a digit as he awaits Atlas's return with the apples. Is it your contention that Heracles does no work? Achieves nothing?"

"Holding a heavy object stationary means there is no transfer of energy," states the hum truculently. "Heracles did not work. He worked when he diverted the river to flow through the Augean stables to clean them out, and he worked when he struggled to bring the three-headed dog Cerberus up from Hades, but he did not work when he held up the sky, only when he transferred it back to Atlas." Then as if speaking to itself again, the hum adds pessimistically, "I must explain to them that the transfer of energy is not transfer of momentum. And then there is . . . ah, why me? Wrong again!" Its wail is drowned out by the sound of a hammer from a nearby house where a carpenter is driving a peg into a new ceiling beam.

When the sound momentarily stops, Lycos asks pointedly, "Do you work?"

There is a silence. "Work can also be defined more generally as exertion of strength or faculties to accomplish something. I have looked it up in my online dictionary."

"At least that is a more usable definition," retorts Lycos, lifting his cup and indicating to the servant that he would like it refilled. "Show me your accomplishments."

"I am even more confused than before," grumbles Kish loudly over the hammering that has commenced again. "Thus far, Michal has suggested that good work is done when there is a longing in the heart, a desire to worship God even if there is no time to worship, which aligns with what you have written, Koheleth, that '*whatever your hand finds to do, do with all your heart.*' Dreela has stated that humans and other sentient creatures are often forced against their will to work. While the hum over the door has put forth the idea that work must be measurable. Nothing holds together."

"Are you not really questioning why all of life is the way it is?" asks Hemlinsu, directing the question not at Kish but at Koheleth. "In Eden, humans are given everything they need, although Adam is assigned the task of tending the garden. But once Adam and Eve are expelled, their survival is dependent on the sweat of their brow, in other words, work."

"Even those people who are so wealthy they don't have to work physically are reliant on those who do. It is a long ladder of oppression," adds Targitaos. "Let me read from Koheleth's fifth chapter: '*If you see a person oppressed in a region, and justice and rights denied, do not be surprised, for one official is watched by a higher one, and over them both are others higher still. The profit of the land is for all. The king himself is served from the field.'* Which brings us back to Dreela's griffins. The lesser griffins are forced to work for the greater griffins, who, I presume, work for overseers who work for administrators who work for rulers."

Lycos leans forward and puts his elbows on the table, squinting his watery eyes in an effort to make out Dreela's face. "So Herodotus, that old untrustworthy rogue of an historian, was right about griffins who guard gold dug from the earth! I have long thought he was embroidering the truth."

"Herodotus embroidered a little, as he did with so many stories," Dreela replies, turning her head toward Lycos with the unblinking intensity of a raptor, missing nothing. "The problem is the griffins live in a land with little else *but* gold, a mountainous place where the soil is very poor and cannot sustain enough vegetation for animals such as deer on which the carnivorous griffins like to prey."

"Amazing! To have a creature walk out of myth into real life. And I, an old man, who had given up believing in chimera!" Lycos chuckles hoarsely, as much cough as mirth. "Is there another kind of griffin? Rather like a dangerous hermit?"

"The rogue griffins. Their behavior is publicly denied but secretly condoned by the griffin leaders, because their existence gives the leaders the added power of oppression by means of fear. Recently the love of gold of these rogue griffins has grown too great, turning them into loners who have retreated to caves where they sleep on huge piles of glittering treasure, always with one eye half open to watch for thieves. The Arimaspoi, about whom Herodotus also wrote, put their children to bed at night with stories that warn them about not wandering too far from home and what to do if they should suddenly hear from the direction of the mountains a kind of wailing on the wind that is the sound of great wings."

"Your explanation of griffins is germane to this discussion as is your mention of the use of fear as a means of control," breaks in Koheleth, glad that the hammering has finally stopped and he does not have to compete to be heard. "So let me turn to the section of the scroll that you read earlier, Dreela, because it has three levels, all related to work and oppression. The first, as you pointed out, deals with the relationship between groups of people or sentient creatures, be they nations, societies, races, tribes, clans, or greater and lesser griffins, and it has to do with the evil that comes from

The Tears of Oppression

an imbalance of power. The second level, which you did not read out loud, is on the relationship between individuals. '*Then I saw that all toil and all skill in work come from one person's envy of another.*' Among humans, rank and privilege count for more than we care to admit. One man wants to have greater possessions than another man, even if that man is his brother; to have a finer house, a better team of horses, so that his status will be higher when he gathers with other men at the gates of the city. One woman is envious of another woman's beauty, so she weaves herself a magnificent robe and darkens her eyes with kohl to make herself more attractive. There is barely a human relationship, no matter how loving, that is clean of the taint of envy."

"So it has been since the day Cain killed Abel—whose name incidentally is the word with which we started, *hevel*, being worthless, vanity, nothing, mist," points out Michal. "And the reason for the killing was because Cain was envious that God preferred Abel's work and offering over his. But there are people who work simply for the betterment of others, although even they long to be appreciated for their efforts and are hurt when recognition is given to someone less deserving. And oppression, often very subtle, is the result of this endless competition among us."

"To quote Menahem, it can even be disguised as love. And thus we come to the third level—that of the solitary individual who has no family, but who keeps working hard, piling up riches for himself, finally asking the question, '*for whom am I toiling depriving myself of good?*' No one benefits from this man's work, not even himself, because he is obsessed. As soon as he buys one field with his hard-earned money, he fixes his eyes on another field. The ruby the size of a lentil he bought this morning looks cheap compared to the ruby the size of a grape he spots this afternoon gleaming on the finger of another man. Nothing he possesses has meaning except to be replaced by something else: '*whoever loves money never has money enough, whoever loves wealth is never content with his income.*'"

Suddenly there is the sound of a small *ah*. Koheleth looks down the table and sees that Menahem and the child are huddled together over the child's wooden tablet that is coated with a layer of bees' wax into which shapes have been incised with a stylus. They are oblivious to the on-going discussion. The child's face is glowing and Menahem is quietly repeating the Hebrew word *tov*, meaning good, and patting him enthusiastically on the back.

Koheleth clears his throat to get their attention. Neither the boy nor Menahem look up, continuing to bask in some kind of small shared triumph. Koheleth clears his throat a second time, waiting until Menahem finally notices. "May I ask what you are up to?" asks Koheleth politely.

"Proving one of Euclid's propositions."

Koheleth's eyebrows arch in surprise. "And how is the boy doing?"

"Very well, considering that his understanding of Hebrew is slight and his knowledge of mathematics rudimentary." Menahem's face is much less tense than it had been. He uses his thumb to smooth out the wax, and draws several shapes, arrows, and lines on the tablet with the stylus. Then he moves the tablet toward the boy, who, unmindful of all the people watching him, looks at it as if he has been offered a piece of sesame candy. "He is about to try and solve a problem involving triangles. I expect it will keep him busy for a while." The child leans his upper body over the shapes as if he were a bird about to incubate an egg, his black curls hanging down on each side of the tablet.

"Continue then," Koheleth nods gravely, although his eyes smile. "And perhaps later the boy can show me what he has discovered about calculating infinity. By dinnertime, I expect you will have him figuring out the square root of two."

"I have a downloadable program for non-Euclidean geometry the boy may use," says the hum whose systems seem to be operating properly again.

"That is kind of you, perhaps after our meal," Koheleth says vaguely, having no idea what the voice means by non-Euclidean geometry. "Now Kish, as to your confusion, I will give you an example that will probably only confuse you more since it has as much to do with the meaning of the word *good* as the word *work*. Let us say that I am a physician and that one day I heal a child of a serious illness. It is a very difficult case and I have had to bring to bear all that I have ever learned in order to cure her. When the child arises from her bed, the fever having left her body, I am filled with happiness, not just for her sake but also for my own because I have used my knowledge and my skill to the best of my ability. If someone were to ask me at that moment if being a physician were rewarding, I would emphatically say yes. I would say further that being a physician made me happy and that it was good. However, what if the child died, and not only that child but many children? Let us say that I am working in the midst of a great plague that I cannot stop. Would I say the work makes me happy? Not at all! It would be terrible work, even though I would do it anyway in hopes that my efforts might save a few lives or at least reduce their pain during their dying."

The Tears of Oppression

Koheleth's heartbeat has become erratic again. He places his hand on his chest, inhales slowly, then exhales through his pursed lips. He feels his heart steady. "But now for one more proposition: What if I have the means to easily diagnose the disease, perhaps a device that could determine the cause of the child's sickness by analyzing a single drop of blood? What if once I know the cause, I have an effective medicine readily available; in fact, it is sitting on the shelf in my office. I would not feel any sense of personal accomplishment in saving the child's life, no matter how potentially fatal the disease, because very little was required of me, and very little was truly at stake. So my point is that good work demands something of me; it demands I use my skills and knowledge. And ultimately good work must have a positive outcome, although how it is measured is beyond our knowing. As I have written, '*As you do not know the way of the wind, or how the body is formed in a mother's womb, so you cannot understand the work of God, who makes all things.*'"

Yet another *ah* is heard, this time coming from Menahem. "You have solved it already! Good work! Good work!" And the boy, his face radiant, throws back his head and begins to sing softly. In the courtyard, suddenly quiet, the very high notes wander up and down their own unexplored scales without the constraint of melody or rhythm, as spontaneous as the sound of the first bird surprising itself with its first song at the dawning of the first day. And all the sages in the courtyard feel a stirring in their hearts as if beautiful numbers are dancing in an immeasurable universe, while on Dreela's circlet, the griffins unfurl their wings.

6

Vanity of Vanities

DURING A LONG BREAK for the noon meal, Koheleth takes his walking stick and shuffles toward the garden beyond the courtyard, seeking some time alone to gather his thoughts for the afternoon session. But time alone is not to be found, for to his dismay he is immediately aware of being accompanied by other beings he cannot see. He senses them as a slow vibration of his eardrums below the range of audible sound, and as a brief disturbance in his field of vision like dimly colored geometric shapes drifting across the inner surface of his closed eyelids.

Most of the invisible beings are non-threatening, but not all. The latter he senses as a splinter under his thumbnail or the jab of a thorn in his side. The thought that there will be people in the future who will use his words for twisted purposes fills him with cold dread, as if ice water is welling up in his chest. His only consolation is that the unseen beings, good and bad, do not exist. They possess the possibility of existence but not the assurance. Some will never be conceived. Some will be stillbirths. Born in a time of war, some will die too young. The fortunate will live in a season to love; the unfortunate will live in a season to hate. All will come into the world with purposes under heaven far beyond Koheleth's imagining.

Now one of the beings starts to speak to him. The voice is no more than the sound made by a small feather drifting down from the sky and landing in the dust, but to Koheleth the voice is audible as if someone were talking—or more like singing—to himself. "Ah, Hebrew! The sacred language. Each letter, from aleph to tav, sacred! When at the beginning of all time and space, God said *'Let there be light,'* the letters themselves brought light into being, sweeping away darkness. So beautiful, so beautiful." The voice sighs contentedly and sings a snippet of melody that Koheleth imagines is accompanied by waving hands and the slight shuffle of feet in a dance step. When the singing stops, the voice addresses Koheleth directly. "And you, my oldest-newest friend, do you know that truth also was there, perching on the shoulders of the letters, just like tiny sparrows making their nests on the beams in the House of God?" Suddenly the voice changes its tone, losing its musical quality, becoming subdued with a tinge of frustration. "Tell us, Koheleth, we who hover here on the edge of existence: How then can Scripture be translated? How can it be *allowed* to be translated?"

"Who are you? And when may be your season in the sun?" Koheleth is relieved that this particular speaker seems friendly, imparting a sense of warmth like a comforting old shawl on a chilly evening.

"I am one of the seventy-two Alexandrian scholars who will translate the Torah from Hebrew into Greek. We will include your scroll, which we will title Ecclesiastes, beginning the work of translation not long after your death. The myth spinners will claim we finish the entire translation in 72 days and that working in total isolation from each other by the pharaoh's command, we will select exactly the same words, as if we were scriveners for the Most High—perfectly reliable takers of dictation. They will call our translation the Septuagint and declare it a miracle, thereby indicating God's blessing on our dubious undertaking, even though the truth will be that the task will take us several generations to complete."

"My scroll is also a dubious undertaking, as you phrase it. The debates of this council are making that all the more clear." Koheleth pauses on the path to try to determine which direction the voice is coming from, but it seems to be coming from everywhere and nowhere, inside and outside. Giving up, he moves his stick forward, feels the ground firm beneath its base, and resumes walking. "You are very fortunate to reach amicable agreement."

"Amicable agreement? Oh no! The debates among us will be as heated as the air in Alexandria, and as lengthy as the Nile itself. Who knew there could be quagmires in Genesis, quicksand in Psalms, and two-headed monsters in Isaiah! Take, for example, the first verse in Genesis as we will translate it into Greek: *'In the beginning God made the heavens and the earth. But the earth was unsightly and unfurnished and darkness was over the deep and the spirit of God moved over the water.'* But what of the Hebrew word *tohu* meaning *without form*. How can *without form* be translated *unsightly*? Does that mean *unable to be seen*, as in *un-sighted* or *immaterial*?"

"Some readers in the future might think it means ugly," remarks Koheleth.

"Something ugly must be visible, or else how would anyone know it is ugly?" the voice replies. "Which brings into my mind a vision of the cloth merchant who will live down the road from me. He will be so fat every chair he sits on will splinter and crash, so he will sit instead on a great sawed off tree trunk in his courtyard, his arms like enormous branches and his fingers like yellow fungi sprouting from the tips."

"Or my sister-in-law with her burned face for whom veils are blessings because they bestow *un-sight*."

"And just as we two in this most visibly beautiful garden are already struggling with the meaning of unsightly, what are we to do with the Hebrew word for *void* which does not mean *unfurnished* as if God forgot to supply the earth with tables and chairs? Such battles we Septuagint scholars will have! Stools will be broken! Plates will be smashed! Ink will be intentionally spilled! It may take us years to reach the second verse of Genesis! Fortunately, to a Jew, nothing is as intoxicating as the intense grappling together to perceive meaning." The voice sighs in pleasure and as if in response a sparrow lands on an olive tree and fluffs its wings. "So when I grow old, I will recall our intellectual battles fondly, especially those with a brilliant sage named Sira. Perhaps you know him. He would be much younger than you but your times on Earth should overlap, at least a little."

"I do not know anyone by that name."

"He began his training at a very early age here in Jerusalem, then was taken while still a small boy to study in Alexandria. Such a gift with languages! So wise! The days of translation working with Sira will be almost the best of my life—surpassed only by the blessed days of my children's births."

"That is so in my life as well; to which I would add the time I met and married Michal. You are not only wise but also kind. Thank you for being here this day, before the seed of your father is planted in your mother's soil and you, who are now without form and void, will feel God's spirit moving over the inner waters of creation." Koheleth continues to walk slowly up the path, stopping to admire a chrysanthemum on which a honeybee buzzes.

"When darkness is upon my own deep and I am surrounded by a human I do not know—cannot know—until the day of our separation—my birth."

"It is strange that in separation, in a little distance, comes the ability to comprehend. Then is unity with God something to be desired? Or would it be better to be able to walk beside each other as friends, or as the psalmist has written, like a weaned child with its mother? This line of thought pertains to translation as well. What part is your thinking, what part is God's? If you feel inspired, does that make your words divine?" wonders Koheleth.

"You ask too many questions, far too many questions, and all at once!" huffs the scholar with a tone normally accompanied by the shaking of a head and the wagging of a finger. But all Koheleth can see is the sudden rustling of a clump of dried grass at his feet as if buffeted by a tiny wind. "Although in the usual flow of time I will learn from you, and not you from me, I will use this opportunity to reverse the natural order. So let me take the last question only, the one that deals with inspiration and the divine." The voice stops as if to organize its ideas, trying to decide how to begin. "Translators cannot abrogate all rights to their own thoughts. That being true, how can any writing—imbued with the severe limitations and self-serving proclivity of the human mind, the human language riddled with swears and lies, the human hand that makes mistakes in copying—ever be truly divine? Yes, there will be moments of inspiration when suddenly one of our Septuagint translators will come up with a felicitous turn of phrase; but there will also be long days and weeks of plodding dullness when the words we choose will be no better than those scribbled in chalk on a placard outside a tavern advertising the day's special of lentil stew, the same meal that has been served every day since the tavern opened during the reign of Rameses II. Forgive my attempt at a joke. May it not be seen as sacrilegious, but I must conclude that frequently our spiritual muse will be quite dull. And always there will be the feeling that we are limiting the meaning, unwisely asserting our own opinions. When the task is finished, I personally will feel both great happiness at its success and overwhelming sadness at its failure."

Koheleth squints his eyes and for a second time scans the air and the garden, but there is nothing to be seen except a slight agitation of the water in the brook. He decides to direct his words to that momentary riffle. "Already here in my generation a translation of Torah is necessary because of the dispersion of the Jews out of Israel as far west as Tarshish bordering the endless ocean and at least as far south as the first cataract in the Nile. In my mind, I see them putting up their tents and driving in their pegs in lands so distant not even a whisper of God's name has reached there. And in those strange places, with the work of the day done and the first star twinkling into view, they gather tired and homesick on the eve of the Sabbath to break bread, drink a cup of wine, and light candles as a small daughter tugs tentatively on the corner of her father's dusty robe. When acknowledged by a hand laid on her head, she asks softly if God is pleased with prayers spoken in Tamil. So I turn back to you the question you just asked. How can a translation be allowed? How can it not?"

"It hurts to say it, for to me it is like eating pig to keep from starving, or crocodile, or swarming insects, or snakes—all unclean to a Jew—detestable. Maybe it is better to starve? But the truth is Greek has become the common language of the lands that ring the Western Sea. Our people are losing their fluency in Hebrew. They say the daily prayers with only partial understanding of what the words actually mean. Such a loss! We have no choice but to translate. Yet it hurts our hearts. All we can do is to leave it in God's hands; that he make sacred what we in our weakness and limited understanding make profane."

"The same thing occurred several hundred years ago during the Babylonian exile, which is why the partial translations into Aramaic were completed. Yet we Jews regained fluency in Hebrew after our return to Jerusalem when the city and the temple were rebuilt and the Torah read aloud," says Koheleth with a rising inflection as if a question mark is hovering at the end of his statement.

"That is so, which gives us hope that ultimately we will all return from Egypt, Babylonia, and from lands beyond the last wave of the sea, traveling on camels bedizened with scarlet fringe and little gold bells. Conquering heroes, riding home in glory."

"More likely we will be carrying our sleepy children on our shoulders while we tug at the ropes of tired little donkeys piled with our meager possessions," says Koheleth.

"At that time perhaps our Septuagint translation will no longer be necessary. How wonderful it would be to learn that it has been laid aside on a library shelf visited only by a tiny red spider. Only rarely, maybe once in a generation, will a scholar who is interested in obscure documents retrieve it from the shelf, blow off the dust, and disturb the spider's descendants who are its rightful owners by dint of their constancy. Sages and translators like to think their work is permanent. Your weakness, your delusion as well, Koheleth. But I pray my work fills a need that is temporary. No less important than a drink of water to a thirsty man, but no more lasting either."

Koheleth reaches down and picks up a pinch of dirt from between the paving stones, then lets it go. "This dirt is our homeland. But there is something in us that wants to wander as well as stay. Before Adam and Eve

Vanity of Vanities

were driven out of Eden, I think they might have been tempted to climb the wall, if there were a wall, to see what lay beyond, testing their ability to survive on their own without the assurance of an always abundant crop of beans and squash. In the perfect garden there would not have been a hungry beetle in sight, not a touch of fungus, not even a rabbit chewing the leaves. No challenges whatsoever."

"And dwelling in Alexandria's congested streets, so narrow in the Jewish quarter I can almost touch the houses on both sides with my outstretched arms, I also have wondered if the workers who were building the Tower of Babel—or closer at hand the magnificent Alexandrian lighthouse—were driven by a longing for more air and space. If I had been one of the workers, I might have greeted God's dispersing curse with excitement at the prospect of exploring the unknown."

"A curse accompanied by the shattering of one language into a multitude of languages, leading in turn to the creation of a new job—yours and mine—that of translator. Which reminds me of another question: Why do you need seventy-two translators, far more than I have gathered here this day?"

The voice laughs and suddenly the water in the brook returns to normal, gurgling over the rocks. "There will be stories told that the head of the Alexandrian library will urge the Egyptian pharaoh Ptolemy to have the Torah translated so it can be included in that vast source of knowledge, like nothing humans have ever seen before. Ptolemy will dispatch an emissary to the high priest in Jerusalem who in response will send six scholars from each of the twelve tribes of Israel, adding up to seventy-two, although the name placed on our work, the Septuagint, indicates seventy."

"I am surprised that you will choose to include my scroll, of all those written since Genesis the most recent and most insignificant. What word will you choose for *hevel*, and will the choice of the title *Ecclesiastes* be unanimous among you?"

"For the word *hevel*, which you want us to translate as mist, we will choose instead *mataiotes*, conveying a vain transitory quality, a pointlessness. And yes, there will be agreement on using for the title the word Ecclesiastes because it means in Greek a civic gathering, such as this very council of scholars."

"Or my council of rabbis who will meet in a beautiful vineyard near the sea in the city of Jamnia," breaks in a new voice. Koheleth stops in the path and observes a small iridescent beetle that has landed on the back

73

of his hand. It lifts its divided outer shell, like two hard wings, to reveal translucent white wings beneath, so delicate they do not look sufficient to the task of flight.

"Each day we will debate whether your book is inspired or heretical. It will be about 350 years from now, nearly a century after the birth of the man some will claim as a messiah, the man who will cause such havoc in our land. At the time, there will be a difference of opinion between two rival schools led by followers of Shammai and Hillel, scholars of immense profundity but markedly different personalities and viewpoints. Shammai—austere and acerbic. Hillel—friendly and compassionate. Sweet Hillel. Who could not love him? A man of peace who taught that compassion is at the center of our faith."

Koheleth is not at all perturbed by the sudden presence of another speaker, because he senses kindness infused with sadness in his voice as he had with the Septuagint scholar. "How did he teach compassion?" he asks as the beetle, having folded its wings, slowly crawls up Koheleth's sleeve.

"There are many stories about Hillel. The one I like best is the time he was challenged by a gentile to explain the Torah to him while he stood on one foot. The gentile had already asked Shammai the same question and been abruptly dismissed. But Hillel replied, 'That which is hateful to you, do not do to your fellow man. This is the whole Torah. The rest is explanation. Go and learn.'"

"I can understand Shammai's dismissal of the man because it is not the type of question that is asked out of a sincere desire to learn, but rather, to annoy. Even so, Hillel's response is far better than Shammai's, taking only a moment to say but a lifetime to understand. Which of these two wise men will defend the inclusion of my scroll into the Scriptures?"

"Both men will be dead by the time of the council at Jamnia. But it will be the school of Hillel who will prevail over the school of Shammai. The students will recall that while he was alive he had told his followers as they walked together through a wheat field, deep in conversation, that your scroll does not, as we say, 'defile the hands.' That means it is not profane because it is the wisdom of King Solomon written when he was an old man, bent with the heavy weight of his failures and sins. However, at Jamnia, even though Hillel's followers will win, there will be no binding resolution that everyone will be required to sign or else risk censure. The way of the Jews, as my forbear from Alexandria has already mentioned, is intense engagement with Torah and sharp debate among ourselves, stretching over generations and generations."

"So also in this council of scholars. Conflicting opinion is not to be feared; indeed, it indicates the possibility of an unplumbed depth of meaning—infinite depth. Most of the scholars here today, but not all, sadly not all . . . " and Koheleth thinks first of Menahem and then of Djadao, " . . . are mindful of their own intellectual shortcomings, asking themselves whether the failure to comprehend might be their own." He gently nudges the beetle off his sleeve and onto the side of his walking stick.

"We at Jamnia will agree. That being the case, how can we condemn a passage of Scripture or even an entire book?" adds the voice. "Although it is true that to some rabbis at the council, the acceptance of Ecclesiastes will be based on its attribution to King Solomon, to other rabbis and scholars it will be your unwavering viewpoint that resonates in their hearts, for they will have seen in their lifetimes the fissure of Judaism by the followers of Jesus—that is his name, Joshua—the man claimed as a messiah. And they will have seen the complete destruction of the temple by the Romans, leaving only part of the foundation of the western wall."

Suddenly a great pain surges in Koheleth's heart and he clutches his chest. He staggers to a nearby bench and slumps down heavily, overwhelmed not just by the pain but by the horrifying visions in his mind. He sees siege towers being built outside Jerusalem, and an invading army camped on the Mount of Olives; he sees soldiers swarming through the breach in the wall, and fire climbing the curtains of the temple; he sees a scribe crushed to death by a falling beam, a child in flames screaming as she runs naked from her home, and people crucified in twisted positions on a forest of crosses covering a scorched Judean hill. "What you say," he gasps after a few minutes, "for me, it is like having my tongue cut out, like trying to walk without feet. How many times must my beloved Jerusalem be destroyed?"

The Septuagint scholar answers in a voice that is hushed and choked. "It will be as Isaiah predicted: *'Your holy cities have become a wilderness. Zion has become a wasteland. Jerusalem a desolation. Our holy and beautiful house where our ancestors praised you has been burned by fire and all our pleasant places are ruins.'*"

Beads of sweat glisten on Koheleth's brow and he leans forward to make it easier to breathe. "Yet we . . . go . . . on . . ." Again Koheleth tries to inhale and exhale slowly, squeezing his eyes shut and bending all his powers of concentration inward. But the disturbing visions continue to assault the eyes of his mind. This time he sees nothing where Jerusalem once stood; no buildings, gardens, trees, people. All he sees is a wasteland across which a dog prowls, hunting for food among scattered foundation stones. For at least five minutes, there is silence.

When the rabbi begins again, his voice is filled with concern. "You are a little better?"

"Yes, a little better." Koheleth says weakly. "*But the sun and the light and the moon and the stars grow dark and the clouds return after the rain.*" He wipes the sweat from his brow with the sleeve of his robe. "Those words are from the end of my scroll."

"You will live long enough. This, at least, I have been given to know. As you have written, '*before the pitcher is broken at the well and the dust returns to the earth as it was.*' I know your scroll well."

A little color returns to Koheleth's ashen face. "*And the breath returns to God who gave it.*" He begins to relax. "But not yet?"

"No, not yet. You will not die while talking with us in your garden," says the Septuagint scholar, sounding like a solicitous physician leaning over the bed of a very sick patient. "There is still time for you to remind us that the limitation of knowledge in the face of God's inscrutability does not mean that seeking knowledge is futile. What is essential is to value knowledge correctly."

"There will be a midrash written in regard to your scroll—the scroll named Ecclesiastes," says the rabbi. "I quote it for you: 'In one sense there is a benefit in failing memory; if a human's memory did not fail, there would be no study of the Torah.' From this midrash, it follows that there is a benefit in the limitations of knowledge, because it requires people to work at learning. They have to struggle, and in that struggle is the very nature of humanity. They have to go on. So must you."

Koheleth straightens up on the bench, but his voice is still strained and the look in his eyes is not of relief but of gritty resolve. He attempts to smile but manages only a fleeting upturn of his lips. "Your midrash is good for my heart. Do you have another story equally healing?"

"I will tell you a story also from midrash, written down long after my death but circulated well before. It is about how we know what we know; it may make you laugh, or at least smile, both laughter and smiling being medicines most helpful to the heart when taken at the right time and in the right dosage. Once there was a Persian who wanted to be instructed in the Jewish faith, so he went to see the great Rabbi Judah Hanasi. At the beginning of

Vanity of Vanities

the session, the rabbi showed him the first letter of the Hebrew alphabet, but immediately the man began to argue, asking how it could be known that the letter is called aleph. So disgusted did the rabbi eventually become with the man's insistence, he threw him out. So the man went next to Rabbi Samuel and asked the same thing. Rabbi Samuel pinched the man's ear very hard, and he cried out 'O my ear!' 'How do you know that this is an ear?' asked Rabbi Samuel. At that answer the Persian was pleased and went on to study diligently." The voice stops and then asks in concern, "How is your pain?"

"Decreasing. I have had these spells before, but in the last few days they have been occurring more often and are much more severe." Koheleth leans his chin on the top of his walking stick, observing the little beetle that is still wandering about. "I like your Rabbi Samuel. When will he live on this earth?"

"The second century after the coming of the man some will claim as the messiah."

"This is the third time you have mentioned a messiah. What language will this man speak?"

"Definitely Hebrew, Aramaic, probably Greek and a language beginning to spread around the Western Sea called Latin."

"Then will there need to be a translation into Latin, and, if so, who will do it?" Suddenly the beetle lifts into the air on its translucent wings and disappears into the foliage of an olive tree.

"My name is Jerome and I will do it," says another voice as a passing cloud darkens the garden and Koheleth feels the chill he had first felt on sensing the unseen beings. "Vanitas vanitatum dixit Ecclesiastes vanitas vanitatum omnia vanitas." The words sound like a dirge sung in the candle-lit interior of a building made of stone. *"Vanity of vanity, says Ecclesiastes, vanity of vanity all is vanity."*

To Koheleth, it seems as if the speaker is intoning the words on the way to an execution. Images of the limp bodies of men hanging from scaffolds, women flayed alive, and children thrown from parapets sear Koheleth's mind. "When will this happen?"

"I will be born in Dalmatia in 347 Anno Domini and will study in the great city of Rome."

"I have heard of Rome." Koheleth is relieved to be able to recognize something familiar in the stranger's statement. "There is nothing that would recommend it as a place of learning, a backwater, of no account.

I did not even include it on my itinerary when I traveled around the Western Sea as a young man."

Without comment, the voice continues dryly. "For two decades I will wander, studying with the esteemed Didymus the Blind in his school in Alexandria—he who lost his sight as a child but who learned all Scripture by heart and who wrote one of the first great commentaries on Ecclesiastes, although long after his death his works will be condemned and destroyed by the Second Council of Constantinople on account of his abominable doctrine of the transmigration of souls. Such a fool he became! You see, even the brightest scholars can fall prey to grievous error that only fire can purify." He clears his throat of phlegm and coughs repeatedly. "But that will come much later. Following my time with Didymus, I will live as an ascetic so hungry that I will dream of mountains made of fresh bread. Then I will spend time as a hermit in the desert, desperate for conversation, praying the stones will cry out so I will hear words. What I will learn from that experience is that I need the abrasive edge of doctrinal argument to make me feel alive. More to my liking than the years as a hermit will be the time I spend studying Hebrew with a Jewish convert to Christianity."

From the olive tree comes a moan as if a father is wailing for a lost child, his heart fractured into a million pieces. A dead leaf swirls down and lands on the bench. Koheleth picks it up and places it on the palm of his hand, treating it as a thing of great value. However, Jerome does not take notice, so fixed is he on his soliloquy. "In my preface to your book, my commentary on Ecclesiastes, I will write that I followed no one's authority, but translated directly from the Hebrew, adapting my words as much as possible to the form of the Septuagint but only in those places in which they did not diverge far from the Hebrew. Yes, I admit I will refer to the versions of Aquila, Symmachus and Theodotion, but I will endeavor not to turn aside, as I have written, 'against my conscientious conviction from the fountainhead of truth.'"

Koheleth has known several fountainheads of truth that ran dry, turned muddy, or were poisonous. He studies the withered leaf in his hand as if it were a tiny map to the kingdom of God, before letting it flutter to the ground beside the bench. "Is there an exact location of the fountainhead of truth, a place marked with the letter x?"

"The monastery in Bethlehem, the birthplace of our Lord, of course!"

Vanity of Vanities

Koheleth thinks he hears the rap of a wooden dowel being brought down hard on a map, the point piercing a hole in a small village not far from Jerusalem.

"That is where I will work on my translations, in a cell alone, with only a hard bed, a rough-hewn table, my writing implements, books, and a candle. The monastery will be built with funding from a wealthy Roman widow named Paula, a devout Christian who will also establish a convent and a hostel for pilgrims on the same site. She is of an old Roman clan that proudly claims descent from Agamemnon. I will come to know her and her family during the three-year period when I will serve as secretary to Pope Damasus."

"I do not know of Pope Damasus, but Agamemnon, I know of him: commander of the Greek forces in the Trojan War; certainly not Roman. Your Paula has been misled. He killed his daughter Iphigenia to appease Artemis, the goddess of the hunt, and then was killed in turn by his unfaithful and vengeful wife Clytemnestra, but was killed as much by his own high opinion of himself." Koheleth brushes away a wasp that is buzzing annoyingly around his head. "For Agamemnon, at least, your translation rings true. Vanitas vanitatum, Vanitas vanitatum omnia vanitas. I am intrigued by the way the words roll off the tongue, musical but also heavy, like the tolling of an iron bell."

"It will be to Paula's daughter Blesilla that I will read your book, hoping thereby to provoke her to have contempt for this earthly scene, and 'to count as nothing all that she sees in the world'—words I have written. Blesilla will be the one to ask me to write a commentary on Ecclesiastes so that while I am absent from Rome she can read it and come to a greater understanding about the importance of withdrawing from the vain world in preparation for the perfection of Christ and his heaven."

"Withdraw from the world?" Koheleth grips his walking stick with such force his knuckles turn white and the pain again shoots through his chest like fiery arrows, but his voice is steady. "That is not in my scroll. You overlook my advice. Well, to be truthful, it is not *my* advice. I borrowed it from the speech of the tavern keeper in the ancient poem about Gilgamesh. The advice is: to eat your bread with gladness and drink your wine with a good heart, to dress in white, and to enjoy life with your beloved wife."

"No I do not overlook it. I take it symbolically to refer to the Eucharist, the body of Christ being your bread, the blood of Christ being your wine. And as to your beloved wife, she is not an actual flesh-and-blood woman but the church itself! These are the things on which we must set our eyes and hearts. Toward all the rest, we must have *comtemptas mundi*, meaning in Latin contempt of the world, for the world is as defiled as the white stump of a leper. You are the man, Koheleth, who taught me that all things are vain and useless. You are the man." And to Koheleth it feels as a disembodied index finger is pointing at him from the air. "Certainly you know that the things you just mentioned—eating, drinking, dressing well, intercourse, are vapid consolations for an existence of nothingness. We Christians have found a better way through the life and death on the cross of God's only begotten son, Jesus Christ, the messiah."

"Alexander also called himself the son of god. He was given that title by the priest at Siwa, the sacred oasis in Egypt that he visited for the express purpose of being deified. But the god he was referring to was Ammon-Zeus," counters Koheleth. "In fact, the appellation is quite common as is the phrase son of man used repeatedly by Ezekiel."

Jerome doesn't offer a rebuttal as if he does not consider Koheleth's remarks worthy of a reply. He plows on with his sermon. "Therefore, it is toward heaven that we strain, the highest way being celibacy, contemplation, and an ascetic life."

"This messiah of yours, maybe he is not world-denying but is like a joyous bridegroom, a man who is so happy he can't help but dance! We Jews love weddings—the joy of a young man and a young woman celebrating their adoration of each other with their friends. Even if their families are too poor to provide wine for the celebration, even if the bride is as plain as a clay pot, we will drink the water provided and praise it as the best vintage, and we will exclaim that the bride is beautiful. This messiah, perhaps he would be a good storyteller. We Jews love stories! There would be stories of lost coins found, pearls hidden in fields, and a derelict son being reunited with a long-suffering father. I see a messiah who lifts children in his arms and considers himself blessed for the opportunity. We Jews love children! You see, this hypothetical messiah might be able to do all these things because he knows that although life is difficult, indeed even cruel, it is also good, simply good, the Hebrew word *tov*. Were there ever to be such a messiah, there would be no contempt for the world in him. How could there be when the world, created by God, is each morning sustained anew?"

"Yes, I admit that the things God creates can be said to be good in themselves, but compared to the Christ, they are nothing. Vanitas! If I look

Vanity of Vanities

at a candle and am content with its light, what will I do when I see the sun, or in the fullest sense—the son?"

Again there is a moan from the direction of the olive tree, but this time the rabbi from the council at Jamnia speaks. "In the Talmud it is written that in the world to come, a human must account for all the good things—the blessings—that God placed on earth that the human refused to enjoy: the sun breaking through after the rain, the weight of a sleeping child's head resting on his shoulder, the warmth of a wool cloak on a winter night."

As if he does not hear, Jerome continues his soliloquy without responding to the rabbi's comments. "It will not be until I receive a request from my friends Cromatius and Heliodorus, bishops of Aquileia and Altinum respectively, for commentaries on the Old Testament books of Hosea, Amos, Zechariah, and Malachi, that I will begin to translate your book from Hebrew into Latin, the vernacular language. You see, I will become very ill, and although Cromatius and Heliodorus will send funds to help pay my scribes, the work they request will be too much for me. So instead, I will translate Ecclesiastes, Song of Songs, and Proverbs. In a fine fit of insight, I will finish the translations in three days, preserving the flavor of the words and preventing them from going sour."

"Three days? Sounds like a miracle similar to the seventy-two days of the Septuagint translation." Koheleth shakes his head, feeling so exhausted that each word he speaks weighs on his tongue as if it were a rock. "What will become of your translation?"

"Eventually it will be called the Vulgate, meaning common, and will be the Bible of the entire Christian world. But only churches, cathedrals and other religious centers will have copies and only priests and monks will be allowed to read it. Plain folk, most of whom will be illiterate, and who should remain so for their own good, must receive the word of God via the priests who can select what is appropriate, thereby protecting them from error and the fires of hell.

"The phrase *for their own good* sounds more like a curse than a blessing," whispers the rabbi, his voice getting softer and softer. "You have a strange way of twisting the meaning of good."

Again Jerome ignores him. "Eventually Latin will be considered the one and only sacred language, and anyone who translates the Bible into another language will be committing a sin so huge he will be tortured to death. But I will die a normal death in old age after which I will become the patron saint of translators and librarians."

"Let me be the first to offer you congratulations on your appointment as a father-sacred, which is what I assume you mean by patron saint," Koheleth says with a tone as dry as the sand beneath his feet. "What are the responsibilities of a patron saint?"

"We intercede for librarians and translators in heaven, so that God will hear their supplications."

"No doubt that all books be returned on time and that people whisper." Unable to stand anymore of Jerome's ideas, Koheleth puts his hands over his ears and stares at the ground. "Now please, all of you, I must be by myself for a while. I need to sit here on this bench, alone." And suddenly there are no presences around him, no feather, no iridescent beetle, no dried leaf, no tolling bell, only the sound of the brook. Wilted, he lets that sound flow around him and through him, in no rush to resume the work of the day. Not until he feels in his heart the greening of a single leaf does he rise.

7

Eat Your Bread with Gladness

When Koheleth returns from his walk, he is surprised to find that things have not progressed very far, as if his conversations with the Septuagint scholar, the rabbi, and Jerome had taken place in a small eddy off the main river of time. He washes his hands in one of the large clay jars filled with water placed just inside the entry and shakes off the droplets, attempting to shake off as well the haze of disorientation. He feels as if he has been jolted awake to find himself in a familiar place that has turned utterly strange: the door entered a thousand times leads to a hallway never walked; the sunlight slants over a roof from the wrong direction. He limps to his place at the head of the table trying to avoid eye contact so as to avoid as well the need to speak. Slowly his head begins to clear and the world around him resumes its prior form and flow.

The succulent aroma of lentils cooked with onions, and roast lamb seasoned with rosemary fills the courtyard, and Koheleth settles down to eat the food that his cooking staff has been preparing all morning. He is weak from the intense pain that had gripped his chest for several minutes while in the garden, compounded by the lingering discombobulation brought on by his ethereal visitors. He looks around for his head servant (whom he considers a friend) and when he spots him carrying a wooden bowl filled with cooked manioc root to a woman sitting on her haunches near the wall, Koheleth nods his head to him, a gesture of gratitude so small nobody but the servant notices, nodding slightly in return. Koheleth is grateful not only for his own bowl of lentils and lamb but also for his servant's solicitude toward his guests. How to soak manioc root for several hours so as to remove its poison is not common knowledge in Israel. With a look of pleased surprise, the woman reaches out a blue-tattooed hand and takes the manioc from the servant. Then quietly Koheleth says the blessing over his own food. "Blessed are you, God, Lord of the universe, who causes to bring forth bread from the earth." Then to that blessing he adds another: "Blessed are you, God, Lord of the universe, who causes people to bring forth small acts of kindness that can make a stranger feel at home, and an old man feel alive."

Having eaten their food quickly, the boy and Sarah are playing with the yo-yo in the corner of the courtyard, taking turns trying to get it to climb up and down the linen string, attempting to snap their hands upwards just at the moment that the discs almost touch the ground as Hemlinsu had demonstrated. At one point, the boy abruptly stops the movement and runs the string between his fingers, looking at it carefully as if for tiny knots. Then he examines the two red discs as if he is wondering what makes them move: their round shape? their smoothness? their size? their weight?

The children's play reminds Koheleth of his boyhood fascination with the transit of the sun, traveling west during the day, then somehow returning to the east during the night. At the age of six, he had speculated about it being hauled back to its starting point by ropes attached to enormous pulleys operated by elephants. No hypothesis he could come up with, no matter how absurd, could be discarded out of hand. In fact, absurdity tended to lead to fruitful areas of youthful inquiry, such as exploration into how pulleys actually worked. With his uncle's assistance, Koheleth had rigged ropes from his window across the courtyard to his uncle's window. Then he had attached a small wooden cage in which rode his intrepid sand rat who made many precarious trips, swinging out across space. Even the topic of the care and feeding of elephants (an animal about which Koheleth had only heard) became the focus of serious investigation, although there was little information available. His uncle, who was usually instrumental in fueling Koheleth's imagination and providing raw materials for his experiments, could only come up with a medallion from the time of Alexander that showed a warrior battling a war elephant. In a way, that medallion turned out to be better than an animal husbandry text because it peaked Koheleth's interest in military strategy, which in the overall scope of his life was far more important than learning how to feed elephants.

Watching the children play helps drive from Koheleth's mind the distasteful feelings he had experienced while talking to Jerome. He dips a piece of bread into the lentil stew and is reminded of the words he has written and that he recently quoted to Jerome *"Eat your bread with gladness,"* to which Jerome had replied that one should have contempt for the world. How could it be so? How could he have contempt for the lentils in his bowl that were planted by a farmer, watered by God's hand, harvested in the warm light of late summer, brought into the market on the backs of donkeys, where they were sold to a member of his staff, then simmered over a slow fire just a few hours earlier, the cook occasionally stirring them, then tasting a spoonful, adding a little more pepper, a little more salt? Where was contempt for the world supposed to start?

Koheleth glances again at the boy who is carefully rewinding the string, looking quizzically at the ground as if to ask what force is pulling the discs downward as Koheleth had once asked what made a fig fall from the branch, instead of rise into the air—a conundrum that had led Koheleth to drop numerous items from the top of the courtyard wall—but not his sand rat—to see what he could learn about the nature of falling objects. He watches the two children talking intently, their heads close together, and their hands moving with their words. He wonders to what degree they understand each other, oblivious to the adults around them, caught up in their own experimentation with the angle of their hands in reference to the plumb line of the string, all mysteriously connected to natural laws that seemed to hold as true for a small toy as for the entire universe.

Suddenly the thought occurs to Koheleth that he should ask Sarah to teach the boy Hebrew instead of Michal or himself, for they are so old that they are out of touch with the world in which the two children play, a world that knows thus far only the season of spring. Like her grandfather, Sarah is inquisitive, although whether she will be able to maintain that attribute when she becomes a woman is problematic. If she takes on the responsibility of teaching the boy, it might be beneficial to them both. Koheleth resolves to give it some thought immediately after the meeting. Encouraging young scholars, pushing them beyond themselves, nudging them toward new dimensions of understanding, are things that Koheleth can still do, not needing physical strength or mental agility to listen, probe, and praise. One thing he can no longer do is wait.

Koheleth is not the only one who has been observing the children; so has Hemlinsu, and now it comes over to them, takes the yo-yo and ties a small loop in the top of the string. Then it demonstrates how to put a finger through the loop, which apparently provides greater control over the movement of the discs. Under its tutelage, the children take turns. When they get the discs to ascend and descend smoothly, their laughter is spontaneous and Hemlinsu claps them on their backs in praise. Several people are watching and soon the yo-yo is being passed around. Even the woman with the blue tattoos takes a turn, giggling in an embarrassed but pleased way when she gets it to work on the first try.

The boy fascinates Koheleth, particularly the way he becomes entranced with whatever he is learning, his dark eyes glittering like obsidian, for example, when he was working on the geometry problems that Menahem had given him during the morning session. That a math class had been conducted openly in the midst of such an august conference does not bother Koheleth at all. On the contrary, it pleases him, because one of the chief topics in the scroll is the nature of knowledge of which the child's intense curiosity is a perfect example. Even with the language barrier, he appears to intuitively grasp what is required, possessing what the Hebrews call insight, having elements of focused discernment and keen awareness that far exceed rote memorization. In fact, it is that aspect of the boy's intelligence that led to Koheleth's decision to have him attend, although the inclusion of a small child—brought to Israel as a slave but being treated like a beloved grandson—made no sense. Koheleth is as rational as a man can be, yet he knows how to appreciate the inexplicable, and has never been afraid to act on impulse.

The boy himself looks to be five or six years old by his height, and the details of his life are unknown, not even the circumstance of his being sold into slavery. His family could have sold him during a time of famine; he could be the booty of war, swept up by soldiers sacking a village; or he could be nothing but livestock, born to a slave mother and raised to be sold, no different than a lamb in the market. Koheleth does not even know his name, nor does he want to impose one on him, preferring to use whatever name already belongs to him. The boy himself has not divulged it, even though he has been given the chance. Koheleth has used signs, pointing at himself and saying his own name over and over, and then pointing at the boy and waiting for him to respond in kind, except the boy has remained enigmatically silent, not intransigent, just silent, to the point that Koheleth has wondered if he has a name. Again Koheleth thinks of the passage about the kingdom of Cush in the scroll of Isaiah, wherein God is so quiet Isaiah compares him to shimmering heat in sunlight—an apt description of the boy.

Curiously, the boy's muteness does not extend to his singing of highly complex wordless melodies often accompanied by the clicking sound that seems to come from the back of his throat, as well as a high whistling, almost a keening. It also does not explain why he sings not only during the day but sometimes deep in the night when he should be asleep, always with a wistful seriousness, as if he were trying to summon a god gone missing, or a dead parent, much loved and deeply longed for.

"Excuse me, Koheleth, for interrupting your meal, but I must talk to you." As the voice brusquely breaks into Koheleth's reverie, he sees Djadao bending over him as if to speak in whispered confidence. His face reminds Koheleth of a loaf of uncooked dough, puffy and pale, with small close-set eyes. "I think you should send the boy away. Also the girl. They are too young and, with their playing, have no place here. This council is far too advanced for such as these."

"I think that they are far too advanced for such as this council," replies Koheleth calmly, stressing the word *they* before taking another bite of the stew.

"They add nothing to the discussion." Djadao mops the sweat from his brow with his sleeve. "Furthermore, Menahem's working with the boy on mathematics during the morning session was highly distracting. As to Menahem..."

"What a welcome addition!" Koheleth says wholeheartedly, intentionally misinterpreting Djadao's tone of malediction as one of affirmation. "Insanity opens up a dimension of unpredictability in the idea of human understanding. But I admit I did not know how to incorporate it in my scroll other than to write about fools and folly, and those are very different from insanity. To me, fools are not intellectually deficient; no, no, they can be quite smart. They are morally deficient, ignoring facts unless those facts align with their preconceptions of how things are or should be. And they never think through the full ramifications of their ideas. Not that any of us do that to the degree we should." Koheleth moves over on his cushion. "Please sit down, Djadao. It is hard for me to talk to you when you are standing and I am sitting."

Djadao awkwardly lowers himself, puffing as he does so. "Menahem also ignores the facts."

"Would you like some olives from my own grove? Very good harvest this year." Koheleth hands him a bowl piled high. "I would not use the word *ignore* in reference to Menahem. To ignore something implies you are making a choice. And Menahem, at least as he was—not as he is right now—did not have a choice. He did not have the capability—the freedom—to choose. On the other hand, the fool can choose, and what he chooses is not to see, not to know, because knowing makes him vaguely uncomfortable. But does he really have the power to choose? That is a question worth asking. I have known a crafty ruler who cultivated foolishness among his people because it made them easier to manipulate into doing his will. But no ruler would cultivate madness in his people. Madness is its own ruler and writes its own law."

With a shrug of annoyance at Koheleth's philosophizing, Djadao grumbles, "You think Menahem's playing with the boy indicates he is in his right mind? That he is making a rational choice? When in the face of wise counsel advising you against it, you invited him to join your staff after he killed your son, he appeared at first to be normal. Have you forgotten how changeable he became? One moment helpful, the next flinging a scroll across the room. His behavior this morning does not guarantee his behavior this afternoon."

"Nor does yours," replies Koheleth pensively and a little sadly, "nor does mine." He takes an olive from the bowl, eats it, and places the pit on his plate with great deliberateness. "What really matters to me is that he has come back. All those years ago, it was as if he were my son demanding his inheritance from me—not of money, but of ideas, of spirit. Ever since the day he stormed out of this house and headed for the wilderness by the Dead Sea, I have been standing at the window casting my gaze toward the rising sun in hopes of seeing him return before I die."

"Good riddance I say! Twice before Menahem has hurt you. More than that—has *crushed* you. Why risk a third time? How can you even use the word *son* in regard to him when he left yours lying bleeding to death in the dust of the road?"

Koheleth is surprised by the passionate vehemence of Djadao's questions for which he does not have adequate answers, at least not ones he can easily slip into words that would in any way be convincing, because his answers have to do with a shift in the time for every season—a shift so subtle that only a human returned to his right mind, a day-dreaming child, and a dying old man would notice it. It had to do with joy. No celebration had planted that overwhelming feeling in his heart, no public honor had watered it. It came of its own, unbidden and unburdened. And in the same way he had forgiven Menahem.

"I remember," Koheleth says in a cracking voice. "I remember it all. And I am touched by your concern for me, but . . ." Koheleth stops. He clears his throat as if trying to speak past a lump. "You bring up the matter of the child. In fact, I was just thinking about him, not whether he should stay or go, but what to call him. Maybe in the boy's culture, there is no such thing as a personal signifier—a name. Or maybe, as in the Egyptian legend, he was raised by women with their tongues cut out so that the pharaoh could learn what first word the boy would speak on his own, thereby revealing what was the oldest naturally occurring language on Earth."

Djadao thrusts his hands into the voluminous folds of his robe and doesn't reply right away, realizing that Koheleth has not responded to his concerns, and is in fact sidestepping them. "I would argue the oldest language is Sanskrit."

"And I, of course, would argue Hebrew."

"The writing on the leaf you gave me is an ancient form of Sanskrit. Which leads to a related issue. At least half of the people you have summoned to this gathering are from cultures with no written languages. Of what importance is a shaman from a village built on stilts over a crocodile-infested river?"

"Oh, then you have spoken to the man who interprets the will of anacondas and speaks with liana vines. Fascinating. I appreciate his coming so far during a difficult time of the year, just before the young men's initiation rites that require so much of his concentration."

"And why did you summon the woman from the frozen land, the one who spoke of mist forming over the ice? What is she to do with a scroll? What is her worth to you? Do you expect her to stand before her people after they have killed a walrus and recite the words 'mist mist all is mist and a striving after wind?'"

"I summoned them, but I didn't demand they come. And I don't know what to expect of them now that they are here. As I said to Ayonwentah last night, I am the beneficiary. I am in their debt. They are not in mine." Koheleth takes another olive from the bowl and rolls it between his fingers as if studying its shape. "Tell me, what were the words written on the palm leaf I gave you? They are from the Rig Veda, are they not?"

Djadao hesitates, as if he is pondering the meaning of the words for the first time. "Let noble thought come to me from all directions."

"Yes, those are the words. *All* directions—not just the horizontal ones of north, south, east, west, but also up and down, in and out, physical and spiritual—all," says Koheleth firmly.

"Still the boy, by dint of his age alone, does not belong here," insists Djadao, but with less conviction as if beginning to question the worth of his arguments.

Koheleth detects the slight shift in Djadao's tone. "I'm not sure anyone belongs here, including myself," he replies wryly. "We are all chasing after wind. But I can tell you one thing: I do not intend that my scroll be read only by old sages. It must not be some esoteric document that a male must be forty years old before being allowed to unroll, and only then if he has thoroughly studied the Pentateuch and has the life experience to understand what he reads. My scroll must be open to all. Even if they are too young to understand it, yet they must not be misled by it either. And that is part of my reasoning for having the children here. Until the boy came, I never really understood Isaiah's beautiful passage about the peaceable kingdom: *'the wolf shall dwell with the lamb, the leopard shall lie down with the kid, the calf and the lion and the fatling together, and a little child shall lead them.'* How in God's kingdom could a child lead, I asked myself. Now I know that the wise adult will be led in all his decisions, first and foremost, by what is good for the most vulnerable, not what is good for the rich and powerful. He will let his mind be led first by the welfare of the child, next by the welfare of the adult, and lastly by his own welfare."

Koheleth signals his head servant and as he watches, the bowls are cleared from the tables, and people are courteously directed to return to their places. "Now, Djadao, if you don't mind, we must begin the afternoon session or we will never finish by nightfall. We are already running behind. For now, the boy stays. Sarah stays. Menahem stays. And I would be grateful if you would also stay. You are an important part of this gathering—more than that, an important part of my life. Do you think I would have given you the leaf were that not so?"

Djadao hefts himself up from the cushion with a puzzled expression, as if he has been gripped by an insight that has shaken scales from his eyes. As he takes his place, he turns and bows slightly, and for the first time in many years, there is no bitterness in his face.

Koheleth scans the room to make sure everyone is ready to begin again. The only change in the arrangement from the morning is that Alithemata has fallen asleep and is taking up the space of two. No one bothers to wake him. The boy has settled down next to Alithemata and is leaning his head against the monk's great bulk as if preparing to take a nap himself. Koheleth is envious. He would also like a nap, one of the fine pleasures in which an old person is allowed to indulge, but he must withstand the temptation to become drowsy. "I would like to start the afternoon session by reading a true story I tell in Chapter 9, verses 13 through 16," he begins. "I know that Hemlinsu has said I sometimes compress my information too much, and as a result, I confuse readers. This section may be a case in point. '*I have also seen this example of wisdom under the sun, and it seemed great to me. There was a little city with few people in it. A great king came against it and besieged it, building mighty siege-works against it. Now there was found in it a wise inhabitant, and he by his wisdom delivered the city. Yet no one remembered that inhabitant. So I said wisdom is better than might; yet the inhabitant's wisdom is despised, and his words are not heeded.*'"

"I saw this myself many years ago, or at least the outcome, because by an accident of timing, I ended up in that little city on my way to Persia. The siege was over, the enemy gone, but the devastation surrounding the city was total. Not a single blade of grass or a stick of wood remained where once there had been wheat fields. I was told by the city's ruler that for months on end the plain had been covered with enemy soldiers, war horses, tents, and battering rams, all waiting for the city to capitulate. Then one morning, the soldiers on the city's wall heard a great commotion and to their amazement as they watched, every tent in the enemy's camp was taken down and every piece of gear packed away. By nightfall, nothing remained outside the city gates but piles of dung and smoldering ashes from dying campfires. Maybe the enemy king had received disturbing news of an uprising back at his palace and had been forced to return in haste to defend his own kingdom. Or maybe, mystified by the city's ability to withstand the siege, he simply gave up and withdrew. For there was a wise man in the city who had devised an ingenious way to keep the inhabitants supplied with food during the siege. Nobody starved; not one frail newborn, not one feeble elder. Yet during my visit, when I asked the ruler if I could meet this remarkable man, he had to inquire of one of his advisors what his name was and where he might be found. Why did this incident seem so great to me that I felt compelled to write about it? What struck me was the realization that humans value the powerful leader, the conquering hero. But we do not value the person who *prevents* a disaster from happening."

"That reminds me of an engineer who designed such an impregnable wall for a city in the north that it was never attacked," says Targitaos, gazing off into the distance as if seeing the place. "That wall was famous. People came from far and wide to study its construction with its ingenious interlocking stones. Even an earthquake couldn't bring it down. But the engineer? He died a pauper."

"Or a person who demands that drinking water be kept pure, thereby preventing the outbreak of disease," adds Hemlinsu. "Since no outbreak occurs, people see no reason to say thanks."

"Nor is a song sung about the person who builds a fence along the top of a steep cliff that drops away behind the village near where the children play, thereby preventing them from falling to their deaths," says Kish. "Is the builder's name recorded? Tell me where?"

"Koheleth, your story is similar to the one told in the scroll of Second Chronicles about the saving of Jerusalem by King Hezekiah," says Michal. "Perhaps I should tell it."

"Please do," replies Koheleth, "for it was on my mind as well."

"Hezekiah, a king honored in our annals, ordered the Spring of Gihon, Jerusalem's main water-source, diverted from outside the walls into the city by means of a tunnel so that the city could withstand the siege by the Assyrian king Sennacherib. But how could his order be carried out? More than twelve hundred cubits of limestone had to be cut through, and Sennacherib's army was already on the march! From the north couriers galloped into the city carrying word of villages sacked and crops burned. There was not enough time to prepare. Fortunately, there was a wise engineer on Hezekiah's staff who had supervised the quarrying of limestone from underneath the Hill of Ophel, the very hill on which the temple stands. This engineer knew that the hill was not solid but was riddled with natural fissures and caves that he could use to his advantage. Furthermore, he was skilled in geometry and used it to determine the correct direction of the tunnel, which to this day curves 100 cubits beneath the surface. Under his guidance, two teams of workmen began to hew their way towards each other from opposite sides. Remarkably as they converged, each team could hear through the rock the sound of the other's picks. When they finally broke through, the water of the spring gushed around them, flowing into the Pool of Siloam. Then the engineer set the men to work outside the wall of the city, concealing the source of the spring so that when Sennacherib and his army marched down from the north they arrived at a place without water. And so Jerusalem was able to withstand the long siege and Sennacherib had to give up, returning to his own land in disgrace. Not long after, he was murdered by his sons, an ignominious end. But as in Koheleth's story, nowhere is the name of the engineer recorded. He is forgotten. Only King Hezekiah is remembered."

"It is Isaiah who in his prophecy concerning Jerusalem writes, '*You made a reservoir between the two walls for the water of the old pool. But you did not look to him who did it, or have regard for him who planned it long ago.*' Not only is the engineer overlooked, but so is God. No one thought to thank him," says Menahem. "Incidentally, have any of us thanked the powers that create and sustain us for all the things that have *not* occurred this day? Earlier when I was sitting in the fig tree, a small viper, most poisonous, slid over my hand but did not bite."

"And I sensed a powerful thunderstorm passing over my longhouse. Lightning struck a nearby pine splitting it in two, but no one was beneath it when it fell," says Ayonwentah.

"And I know in my heart that the thin ice just beginning to form along the shore did not break under my husband's footsteps," says the woman from the far north who has taken off the light linen robe the servants had given her the night before and put on her fur-lined parka as if in preparation to leave. "But I also know about the scavenging polar bear."

"The panther has caught a baby monkey and is no longer stalking the little girl gathering firewood," says the woman who had been served manioc root for lunch.

"And the engineer about whom I wrote is peacefully tending his fields. No harm has come his way. Nor honors. As we speak, I can see him swinging a scythe in a wheat field as if he had never done anything momentous, thankful in his heart for the commonness of his day and the harvest that surrounds him." Again Koheleth feels exhaustion begin to wrap round him like a mantle, and his next words are drawn out wistfully. "I wish I were more like him . . . letting God be the judge of what . . . matters."

"What is it that your god says matters?" asks Ayonwentah.

"Everything matters," replies Alithemata, having awoken from his nap.

"Most of all the idea of mattering," says Koheleth.

Fondness, respect and sharp regret mix in his heart as he looks around the table, first at Michal then at Targitaos, Hemlinsu, Dreela, Alithemata—all the people who have enriched his long life and whom he will never see again—Lycos, Kish, Menahem. And his new friends: Ayonwentah; the woman who taught him the word for freezing mist. There is not a saint, savior, or Bodhisattva among them—just people upholding the possibility of meaning even as the words they use slither and seethe; upholding each other even in their narrowness and confusion; and upholding the remoteness of the Eternal.

A few people have left already, evaporating like dew. Many will be leaving Jerusalem the next day, returning to their distant homes. In the stables there is a buzz of activity: servants are grooming donkeys, repairing the saddles and bridles of camels, setting a new wooden wheel on a broken cart. In the kitchens, Koheleth's staff is preparing food for long journeys: dried fruit mixed with sesame, jars of honey, bags of dates, packages of almonds, sacks of grain. It is as Koheleth has written in his eleventh chapter: he is sending out his bread on many waters.

Koheleth closes his eyes and allows his mind to calm down. He listens to the ever-present whirl of Saroruha's prayer wheel and the slight vibration from the computer; he listens harder and hears the old donkey pulling up blades of grass in a distant field; he listens even harder and hears the murmur of his blood entering and exiting the tissue of his flesh. But these are all background sounds. When he opens his eyes a moment later, they come to rest on the foreground sound made by the boy who is still leaning against Alithemata's side, wide awake, humming to himself while watching the sky. Koheleth follows his gaze and sees a small gray cloud drift overhead. Is it the first sign of the coming of rain? Is the boy summoning it? Koheleth wonders, and suddenly his mind is clear, as if washed clean by a downpour. "For now, it matters to me that we adjourn for the day. I hope to see you tomorrow morning after breakfast when we will discuss my final chapter on aging and death. If for some reason I do not see you again, I want to thank you, not only for your thoughts, but more so for your presence—being here with me." Koheleth rises from his place and beckons first to Michal and then to Menahem to join him. "There is a much-used expression—to touch one's heart. So sentimental, unworthy of my scroll. Yet now, I can think of no other phrase that describes how I feel." Leaning on his walking stick and putting his other arm through Michal's, Koheleth leaves the courtyard, with Menahem following several steps behind.

They reach his room and Koheleth closes the door behind them. Then he turns abruptly to Menahem while still holding tightly to Michal. "I want you to take the boy with you—back to the community by the Dead Sea."

"I will take him with me, if he chooses to go, but not to the Dead Sea. It is too harsh a place for a child," replies Menahem without hesitation.

"Where then?"

Menahem does not answer immediately. "To Alexandria," he says finally with quiet resolve.

"Of course!" Koheleth is surprised and pleased. "You will do that? Take him to Alexandria?"

"It is the only place where he can thrive, not wither, for when you die, there will be no one in Jerusalem to watch over him as he must be watched, to teach him as he must be taught. Your translators will disperse. Targitaos will return to the Black Sea. Redeek to the steppes. And you, Michal, will retreat with what is left of your staff and the scrolls to your vineyards by the sea to live out the last years of your life. Only in Alexandria will the boy be given the time and chance to learn."

Koheleth hesitates, his brow deeply furrowed. "After all these years, why did you return?"

"One night I felt the grip of a small hand in mine, and for a moment my darkness lifted. I came to seek the small hand. Today I found it."

"You are well in your mind?"

"My mind is like a burned over field. The fire is out."

"I ask you again. You are well in your mind?"

"I am well in my mind."

Koheleth's face relaxes and he lets go of Michal's arm. He walks to his desk, pulls open a small drawer and removes a bag of coins. "Then go. Raise him up as if he were your own son, our grandson. As Isaiah wrote, raise him '*in the spirit of knowledge and the awe of the Lord. His delight shall be in the awe of the Lord. He shall not judge by what his eyes see or decide by what his ears hear.*' Leave first thing in the morning. And take this money for the journey." Addressing Michal, Koheleth rests his hands gently on her shoulders. "Please arrange to send him what he needs on a periodic basis to pay for the boy's tutors and living expenses." Then he turns again to Menahem. "Take a copy of my scroll. Just like the boy, it stands a better chance of survival in Alexandria. And one thing more: I want Djadao to go with you."

But it is not Koheleth who has the last word. It is Michal. "The boy has a name. He is called Sira."

8

Generations Go, Generations Come

"I KNOW YOUR HOUR is late. And mine? Mine has not come, and *will* not come for over a millennium—if it comes at all. But may I tell you anyway of my translation of your book Ecclesiastes into Arabic?" asks a voice tentatively, speaking in Hebrew but with a peculiar accent that puzzles Koheleth, who is lying in bed but has not fallen asleep, his mind still mulling over the astonishing events of the day.

Koheleth props himself up on his arm and peers into the darkness, not at all put off by yet another visitor, but all he can see is the faint blue gleam of a glowworm on the window sill. "My apologies, whoever you are, I do not know what Arabic is."

"The language of the descendants of Abraham and the servant girl Hagar, beginning with their son Ishmael."

"Ah, the second Abrahamic line: a Hebrew father, who migrated from Ur of the Chaldeans, and an Egyptian mother, from whom God also promised to bring forth multitudes. I know Hadad, one of Ishmael's descendants, and an old friend," replies Koheleth, relieved to be able to make a personal connection. "He lives not far from Jerusalem. Are the seeds of this Arabic language that his family will eventually speak planted in our time?"

"Some scholars think that it sprouts from the tongue of the Nabateans, although they and their words are long gone. May I sit down on the edge of your bed? I have traveled far and, though non-corporal, am tired."

There is a soothing quality to the voice that puts Koheleth at ease, unlike the voice of Jerome that grated against his ears. As if chatting with an old friend, he moves his legs over and smoothes the blanket. "By all means." Then he stops suddenly and slaps the bed lightly with his hand. "What a strange thing to say—by all means! I don't know where it came from. Odd phrases have been popping into my head and out of my mouth all day long. Does the word *means* indicate method, as in your bending your knees to sit on my bed? You *do* have knees don't you? Or does the word indicate a middle position between extremes, an average? Since I do not know, please consider it a polite way of saying make yourself comfortable." Koheleth sighs. "It is as if I have opened a chest of languages and little moths of phrases keep flying out." He swats at the air. "Are you seated?"

"By your right leg."

"Good. To return to the Nabateans. They are desert traders carrying frankincense and myrrh, among many other things. Once there were Egyptian outposts in that region dealing in bitumen to be used in the building of the pyramids. And so I deduce that Arabic is akin to what will be called the Semitic languages?"

"Let me show you the Arabic script and you can reach your own opinion." As if Koheleth is King Belshazzar of Babylon, suddenly the fingers of a human hand begin to write, and letters appear like little golden fish swimming up out of the darkness. "Like the Jews, the Moslems take to heart God's, or Allah's—as they call him—command not to make graven images of anything on earth or in heaven. However, the command does not prohibit the making of an alphabet as visually splendid as the arches of the sky or the glittering waves of the sea."

"Most beautiful, but to my eye, the letters only slightly resemble the Nabatean script. I have studied it a little; it is as difficult to follow as their secret trade routes that head into the wild places belonging once upon a time to the Edomites, from the Persian Gulf north to Damascus." Koheleth watches the last of the golden letters vanish as if it had flicked its tail and disappeared into the deep. "Their literature they keep to themselves. I have never been able to acquire a scroll, even when I have offered more than a fair price. Like their sources of water, their scrolls are hidden; so also is their city in a deep cleft."

"You must mean Petra in the Wadi Arabah. According to a story told by the Arabs, it is the place mentioned in the Book of Exodus where Moses struck a rock with his staff and water poured out. Petra has been deserted for generations on generations."

"Yes, Petra. I have heard people call it that, and it is appropriate because the name in Greek means rock. But there is an older name, a secret name, like a term of endearment that a husband uses for his wife when they are alone in the evening, a softer term."

"What were—or are, to use the present tense—the Nabateans like?" the voice asks wistfully. "You have met them, yes? In my era it is hard for me to learn anything of them. Legends of a lost city where they once spoke the language of angels, that's all I hear."

"I don't know much about them, not as much as I would like. The Nabateans trade with everyone but keep to themselves. Intelligent but aloof. No one knows where they come from or where they go. One day a small cloud of dust is seen in the east, then a short time later a long caravan slowly crests the hill and heads in stately fashion towards the gates of the city. Soon there is a great buzz in the marketplace as rubies and cinnamon, silk and almug wood spill from their bags and are spread out on crimson carpets. The next day they are gone, and the markets are dull, with nothing of interest to offer the shopper except some slightly bruised melons. I have had many dealings with the Nabateans, for they know my interest in purchasing unusual things, particularly scrolls, codices, cylinder seals, anything with writing. From the Nabateans, I acquired the palm leaf that Djadao has been studying, to the detriment of his paying full attention to the proceedings of the council. I do not profess to know any of the Nabateans personally, nor, as I have already mentioned, do I know their language well. They are like your golden letters, appearing and disappearing. A peaceful people when their business is not threatened. A warlike people when it is," says Koheleth. "Why do you ask?"

"I am intrigued by the origins of different races and cultures. How do they come to be, and how does that relate to the languages they speak?" On the windowsill, the intensity of the glowworm changes slowly, pulsating from a pale bluish gleam to a vibrant indigo.

"Bioluminescence," whispers Koheleth flatly, noticing the worm.

"What does bioluminescence have to do with language and communication?" asks the voice, sounding a bit confused. "I can take the word apart to get to its meaning: bio meaning life in Greek, and lumen meaning light in Latin, but I cannot see how it relates to the subject we are discussing."

"Another word that flitted from my mouth," says Koheleth, embarrassed by his inability to control his blurting out strange words. "It has a nice sound, doesn't it? Poetic in the way it slides off the tongue. I was looking at the glowworm, and there it was—bioluminescence." He pauses. "Then again, maybe it is not off the subject. I wonder what the glowworm is communicating and whether it makes a difference whether it is male or female. Which relates, you see, in a roundabout way to a question I asked myself earlier today as I was watching Hemlinsu play with the children. How did it come to be—your phrase—that Hemlinsu's tribe uses two language variations, one for males and one for females? Does the duality of the language maintain the duality of the tribe, or is it the other way around? If the female version of the language were eliminated, how would the role of the women in the tribe be affected? Would they perceive of themselves differently? Would the men? I don't think an outsider can have any idea what a culture is really about without learning its language."

"For me, it is essential to learn other languages given the tenuous existence of the Jewish community in Babylonia of which I will be the leader," says the voice. "Understanding the people we are forced to live among is a way to defend ourselves, albeit not a particularly effective one. Furthermore, the Moslems assert that Arabic is a sacred language, as is Hebrew; that it was the language of the Koran that Allah spoke to Mohammad, the language of angels."

"In Hebrew the word *angel* means *messenger*, and they can walk on two feet that get dusty, and they can sit down and share a meal around a fire with men, dipping their spoons into the porridge. In a way, that is what the Nabateans are: messengers. As nomadic traders, the news they carry is often more valuable then their trade goods, such as the first hint that war is brewing between two neighboring countries, or the state of the pharaoh's faltering heart and whether his tomb will be finished in time for him to set sail into the afterlife. But about themselves the Nabateans speak little." Admiring the moonlight that has begun to spill across the floor, Koheleth changes the subject. "You have not told me when you live."

"It is the tenth century of Anno Domini, meaning in Latin the *Year of Our Lord*—not *my* lord, but the three-in-one lord of the Christians, revered as a prophet by the Moslems who are the followers of Mohammad. You see, in my time, it is no longer Greeks and Romans with whom Jews must seek to co-exist but the Franks, the Persians, the Arabs. Tolerance is always a whisper away from intolerance; tranquility is as ephemeral as dew. Between the sword of the Christian and the scimitar of the Moslem, there is no safe ground."

"Then the words I have written continue to be true. Blessings do not always come to the good or curses to the bad." Koheleth leans his head back wearily and folds his hands across his chest. "What else is the same in your world?"

"One issue that has not changed since the days of Rome is the question of what it means to unite rationalism and faith, science and religion. For example, can a person combine a passion for philology, Biblical studies, and Greek philosophy as viewed through an Islamic lens? And should such a person begin by translating the Hebrew scriptures into Arabic—sacred language to sacred language?

"And what will this person's answer be?"

"The answer will be yes and I am the one who will say it. My name is Saadia ben Yosef, the head of the Talmudic academy in Sura, Babylonia. I will be known as a brilliant defender of rabbinic Judaism, but I also will be known as an expert on the Islamic world, having been born in Egypt in 892, studied in Tiberias, and lived in Palestine. In fact, my Arabic name is Sa'îd Al-Fayyûmî, after the area in Egypt where I will be born, not that far from Alexandria, which, as you know, is to the west of the Nile delta, although about the only thing that will be the same from your time will be the lighthouse that will still be standing, a gleaming giant dwarfing the city."

"Over four hundred feet tall! I saw it at the start of its construction." Koheleth sits up straighter, attempting to find a more comfortable position in which to carry on a conversation. "Already the marble stones towered over the harbor on the island of Pharos. Often in the evening when I was worn out from my studies, my head a muddle—particularly if I had walked that day through the gardens with Euclid, whose explanations of geometry were scintillating but exhausting—I would go to the harbor to see how the foundation had progressed. There was usually a cool breeze, and with the day's work done, the smell of molten lead from the braziers no longer hung in the air. I would stand on the wall and look across the sea as the sun set in a red fire on the waves, feeling the history of all Egypt behind me, its origins lost in the mist of time. How else to say it but as I have said it? '*Mist mist all is mist.*' That was long ago. I never returned to see the lighthouse finished."

"The Pharos," sighs Saadia with admiration. "One of the wonders of the world, although by my time, the fire at the top, reflected by mirrors, will no longer be lit, and earthquakes and great waves will have loosened some of the stones. You mentioned lead. What was it used for?"

"The mortar—all lead if I remember."

"I recall seeing a thin bluish line between the blocks. I wonder why they did not use regular mortar or the bitumen you mentioned as being traded from the area near Petra. The engineering of the Egyptians puzzles me."

"It puzzles and amazes! We Jews have had our engineering triumphs but nothing like the Pharos or the Great Pyramid at Giza."

"I will climb to the top of the Pharos when I will be a small boy not much older than six. On the first landing there will be a crowd of food vendors selling pomegranate juice in clay cups. Also for sale will be copper medallions with the image of the lighthouse embossed into them. How I want to buy one! How I want to carry it in the fold of my robe so I can pull it out and show it to the boys at shul; but my father will say no, that it is a waste of money."

"It is strange that something that you wanted as a child but did not get survives longer in the mind than if that object had been in your possession. The same is true for lost items, such as the little gold ring my sister gave me that I carelessly lost in the sand," recalls Koheleth, touching his index finger as if the ring might still be there.

"Or the leather ball thrown by accident over the wall and scooped up by the sultan's child," replies Saadia plaintively.

"Or the beautiful young woman glimpsed in an open doorway, the breeze playing with the hem of her skirt. An old man's mind is a jumble of lost things, missed opportunities, and disconnected scraps." In the corner of the room a cricket begins to chirp sweetly. "We are getting off the subject again, although to be truthful, I am not sure what the subject is. Tell me more of the Pharos. And why don't you treat it as a memory as well and use past tense with me. That way at least our words, although not our lives, are in the same timeframe."

"Thank you. It is difficult to speak in the future tense about the past, or to speak in the past tense about the future. Now to what I was—not will be—saying. The steep circling stairs, which narrowed as we climbed higher, terrified me. But when we reached the top—never in my life had I seen so far! I told my father that the lighthouse seemed to scrape the sky, that it should be called not House of Light but sky scraper. And then he said something I considered a blessing. 'You are as good with words, my son, as the builders of this lighthouse were good with stone. Your words bring into my mind a city of such buildings—sky scrapers.'" Saadia stops speaking. When he begins again, he is subdued. "Not long after, my father was murdered. So that time at the top of the Pharos is one of my last memories of him."

"A wonderful one. A father's blessing bestowed on a child when it can do the most good is a blessing doubled. Yet the lighthouse doesn't compare to Alexandria's other wonder: its library."

"Alas, that will be burned to the ground about two centuries after your death. The story is that a Roman military leader ordered the torching of the Egyptian fleet trapped in the harbor and that the sparks were carried over the water to the buildings along the shore. But there are other rumors as well, that at later times different religious groups burned it, including the Christians and the Moslems, their reason being to get rid of pagan writings from the past so that they would not defile the true-faith writings of the present. All I know is that the great library is gone. Only the Pharos still stands."

Koheleth looks stricken. "Burned? All of it? Even the smaller buildings and courtyards where the scribes did the copying?"

"All of it."

"It is not a blessing for me to be allowed to glimpse the future, even a future that may not be," says Koheleth. "It weighs on me heavily, as if my bones were held together with the same lead mortar used in the Pharos." He sits up in his bed and pushes a thin strand of hair from his brow as if in so doing he is trying to push the painful images from his mind. "Your father's blessing that you were good with words, tell me, how will that find fulfillment in your life?"

"Besides the Arabic translation of the Scriptures, including your book Ecclesiastes, I will prepare the first Hebrew dictionary titled the *Agron*, meaning collection. I also will prepare a grammar, one of my goals being to keep the Hebrew language from degrading, to nail it down so to speak, so that future generations will comprehend it as we comprehend it. Revelation is important but equal to it is intellectual questioning."

"Nail down Hebrew? Forgive my impertinence, but I hope it finds a way to wiggle free."

"A bad choice of words on my part. Let me use instead the word codify. As we have said, Hebrew is a sacred language. But it cannot be sacred if it keeps evolving, if words are lost or added."

"The word *codify* doesn't set my mind at ease. Oh no! One more strange phrase! I have no desire to have an *easeful* mind." Again Koheleth swats at the air. "Tell me quickly of your other writings before my head is aflutter with moth wings."

"Another work will be my commentary on your book Ecclesiastes as well as poetry in Arabic, using the exquisite alphabet that I showed you. I begin my *Book of Doctrines and Beliefs* by referring to Chapter 7, verse 24 in your scroll. I quote: 'We all seek to probe this distant and profound matter that is beyond the grasp of our senses, and in reference to it, it has been said by the wise king, 'That which was is far off, and exceedingly deep. Who can find it out?' So also I write in my *Book of Creation*: 'For if you ask the wisest among men why does fire tend upward and water downward, or why is the element of air in motion and that of the earth stable, he will not be able to say more than that they were so created and that this is their nature.'"

"Then we agree," says Koheleth. "It is a relief to know that still in your time the history of Judaism is not a history of politicians and military leaders, of palaces constructed and battles won. It is a history of scholars who endure in the face of time and chance. It also pleases me to realize that we scholars can and will converse with each other across the centuries; not as you and I do this night with spoken words but with written words."

"In my book *Sefer Ha-Galui*, I write, 'God does not leave his nation at any period without a scholar whom he inspires and enlightens, so that he in turn may so instruct and teach her, that thereby her condition shall be bettered.'"

Suddenly a different voice begins to speak in a kind of sing-song way that is also plangent, as if small waves were rhythmically rolling up the beach and then washing back down:

> *"With the seed of wisdom did I sow,*
> *And with my own hand labour'd it to grow:*
> *And this was all the Harvest that I reap'd –*
> *'I am like Water, and Like Wind I go.'"*

There is a moment of silence during which the moonlight angles further into the room, casting its silver across the bed, illuminating Koheleth's hand resting on the blanket. "Who are you?" he asks.

"Omar Khayyam, at your service. My last name means tentmaker, the profession of my family, about which I allude in the following quatrain:

> *'Khayyam, who stitched the tents of science,*
> *Has fallen in grief's furnace and been suddenly burned;*
> *The shears of Fate have cut the tent ropes of his life,*
> *And the broker of Hope has sold him for nothing!'"*

"I hear sadness and happiness tangled up with despair. Tell me your time and place, and then perhaps you could recite another," requests Koheleth politely. "I am intrigued by the phrase *the broker of hope*, as if hope were sold in a bazaar by a heartless trader."

"Born in Persia about a century after Saadia's death, in the town of Nayshapur, an ancient caravan city through which Alexander the Great marched on his way east. I will not know about Saadia, but listening to him talk to you, I would have liked to. Forgive me for eavesdropping."

"No need to apologize. Are you also a Jew?"

"No, Shia Moslem. I will grow up to be a philosopher and a scientist who studies cause and effect—one of those simple relationships that undergirds our everyday understanding of how our world works and yet that vanishes when examined closely, as fast as Saadia's golden letters vanished. I will also become a mathematician who writes an algebraic text in which I re-conceive—brilliantly some will say—Euclid's postulates. Also, I will introduce into equations an unknown factor that I will call *thing* in Arabic, the word *shay*. That word will travel in the mental luggage of scholars who will go to Moorish Spain. There it will be spelled *xay*, eventually abbreviated as the letter x, a letter that everyone from school children to academic professors will know well. My sweet x! The symbol of a number that is *real* but is not yet *real*."

"But you mention in your poem the tents of science, not of mathematics."

"Science is a tent in which mathematics dwells. Any scientist who thinks otherwise is deluded. There is ultimately no difference between solving cubic equations and observing the movement of the planets. Which is to say that I will also be an astronomer, spending years of my life gazing at the heavens, climbing to the top of minarets in the middle of the night to get a better view. Because of the accuracy of my observations, I will be asked to reform the Persian calendar, a most mathematical task that I will accomplish with such precision even the Gregorian calendar far in the future will not be as precise. I will measure the length of the solar year correctly to six decimal places. By the way, all this careful observation and analysis will lead me to the conclusion that the earth revolves around the sun."

"So, too, some of the Greek philosophers and scientists concluded," says Saadia. "But Koheleth writes, '*The sun rises and the sun sets and hurries to the place it rises*,' and those words will be used to defend the idea that the Earth is the center of the universe."

"I wasn't making a scientific statement," asserts Koheleth, surprised that a line of poetry would be so misused. "How could I? As the psalmist writes, '*The Lord has set a tent in the heavens for the sun that comes forth like a bridegroom, like a young man ready to run his race. It travels from*

Generations Go, Generations Come

horizon to horizon and nothing is hidden from its heat.' Tents, bridegrooms, race runners—all metaphoric language, all poetry, not science. Both the psalmist and I were trying to indicate the sameness of everything. That's all. 'What has been is what will be and what has been done is what will be done . . . generations go and generations come but the earth remains forever.'"

"You will not have control over how your words are translated and interpreted, my in-the-past friend. This council of yours will have no effect whatsoever, in fact, won't be remembered, might as well not occur, might not even *be* occurring," says Saadia in a way that is more conciliatory than accusatory. "Some people, such as Jerome, may even interpret your statement about there being *nothing* new *under* the sun as an indication that there is *something* new *over* the sun or spelled another way, *son*, to which women and men must aspire. You see, I admit it, Omar was not the only one eavesdropping. I also was eavesdropping on you and Jerome. However, one thing more must also be admitted: it is not only the Christians who have the capacity to spin your words into an interpretation they find acceptable. When it is a Jew doing the interpreting, what is over the sun is taken to symbolize the Torah itself."

"Of course, the truth is that the universe is no more heliocentric than it is geocentric," says Omar airily. "The earth is not the center, nor is the sun. No one can say where is its center, or if there is a center. *When* it started or *if* it started."

"Which is the point made by Heracleides who conjectured that the heavens do not roll around the earth but that the earth turns on its axis from west to east once a day, and that at least the planets Mercury and Venus might revolve around the sun," says Koheleth, recalling a long discussion with Lycos on the subject. "And that particular conjecture was expanded just recently by Aristarchus of Alexandria who believes that all the planets, including the earth, revolve around the sun, and that the stars are infinitely distant."

Omar breaks in, "My point exactly! And so I have written:

> 'Into this Universe, and why not knowing,
> Nor whence, like Water willy-nilly flowing!
> And out of it, as Wind along the Waste,
> I know not whither, willy-nilly blowing.'

Incidentally, the phrase *willy-nilly* is Edward FitzGerald's creative addition to my second and fourth lines. FitzGerald is my translator. I like the sound of that phrase, almost onomatopoeic, combining will and nil in a way that is darkly playful. And the repetition of w! Like the wind itself, breathing in and out of each line."

"In your words, there are strong echoes of mine."

"Which is why I have come," replies Omar blithely. "*Enjoy wine and women and don't be afraid. God has compassion.*"

Koheleth responds, "*Go eat your bread with gladness and drink your wine with a good heart, for God has long ago favored what you do.*"

"Enough of quoting our words to each other," says Omar, "although I would like to do so all night long. There are many such comparisons that can be made between your writing and mine, but what do they prove? The metaphor of life as a pot that is shattered at death is as old as pottery. You use it, I use it. So what? Likewise, the use of *wind* to indicate the transience of life is probably as old as the word *wind*. Incidentally, have you ever noticed that skeptics who dwell in the borderlands of any religion, be it Islam, Christianity, or Judaism, tend to sound alike. So also do the fanatics; it is my experience that a fanatical Moslem is closer to a fanatical Christian then he is to a moderate of his own faith. And I hate fanatics. They are dangerous fools."

Omar's statement makes Koheleth think of Menahem.

"But let me get to the point: I am not here this night because I am a translator of your book. I am here because I will face the same problem that you do, which is how to be just orthodox enough so as to be able to say heretical things and not become a pariah, or worse, a martyr. My vocations of astronomer and mathematician will bring me fame, but my avocation as a poet will bring threats against my life, because my ideas will run counter to Islamic orthodoxy: no reward in the afterlife—if there is an afterlife— no purpose that humans are capable of discerning, only pleasure in the present, including the fleeting solace of wine, women, and song. In fact, so threatening will be my ideas that my poetry will not become well-known until the nineteenth century, made so by the man I have already mentioned, Edward FitzGerald."

"You sound accusatory toward God," says Saadia uneasily. "Koheleth is not accusatory. He accepts God's sovereignty with reverence while admitting he does not understand. No wonder you will be beheaded!"

"No, I won't be. By a struck of incredibly good luck, I will die a natural death in old age in the twelfth century. Which is quite surprising I admit, considering that in one of my most provocative quatrains, I will write that it is unjust for a man who is predestined to sin to be punished. In fact, forgiveness *by* God of a sinful man must be balanced with forgiveness *of* God for making the man sinful in the first place. In another quatrain I assert that the Koran is a *'lovely old book in hideous error dressed.'* That I will live to old age is all the more remarkable given the fact that I will be employed in the court of a sultan where orthodoxy is obligatory. At one point under threat of death, I will make a pilgrimage to Mecca, not out of personal piety but out of self-protection. You see, I love life. Love it! Its beauty, its brevity. I would not make a good martyr."

"What is Mecca?" asks Koheleth.

"A black stone in the desert around which once in a lifetime a Moslem must walk seven times," explains Saadia disparagingly.

"It is more than you think," replies Omar, dropping his irreverent tone and becoming serious. "No one would say I am a believer, but likewise, no one would say I am not. Mecca is a center of power, be it human, divine or a combination. It is like the omphaloskepsis at Delphi, or Mount Zion that we can see from this window, gleaming palely in the moonlight as if it were drawing the light to itself. One must be careful in mysterious and powerful places, admitting humbly the limits of one's understanding. One must tiptoe."

"In the poems you quoted, you don't tiptoe, you trample. I also have spent my life in the courts of rulers, but I know how to watch my words more carefully than you," says Koheleth. "I give advice to my readers not to '*disparage the king even in your dark room,*' by which I mean not only in the readers' bedrooms when they are totally alone, but in their minds. They should not even think a negative thought about a person who wields power over them because there is the chance that the thought will wheedle its way into words that a bird of the air will overhear and repeat. In another passage, I advise caution when dealing with a king, writing that no one can ask him *why* he is doing *what* he is doing; no one can challenge him."

"What of this man your mentioned? Tell us more about him. I think you said his name is FitzGerald and his language English?" asks Saadia. "Do you mean the Angles who live on a large island west of the mainland?"

"I will speak for myself," says a thin high voice, as if the night wind were vibrating a fine copper wire. "In 1859, two books will be published that will have a strange unsettling effect on my country known as England. Anglia in Latin. Ruled by a queen named Victoria. The books—one scientific, the other poetry—will resonate deeply with each other and will upend our concept of religion, the role of God, and the favored status of humankind in the forward march of progress. The first is Charles Darwin's *Origin of Species* and the second is the *Rubaiyat of Omar Khayyam* translated by me, Edward FitzGerald. At your service."

"You are the second one to use the phrase *at your service*. Omar did also. No one is at my service here, but you are welcome to join the discussion, although I understand little of what you just said, particularly the part about the forward march of progress," replies Koheleth, not even trying to determine the direction from which the voice comes. "How did you who speak English come to translate Persian poetry? And am I to assume that my book, called Ecclesiastes, will have been translated into your English?"

"By a learned man named John Wycliffe and his associate Nicholas Hereford working from Jerome's Vulgate," says FitzGerald. "A most terrible story. I hate to tell it. But I suppose I must." There is a long pause, followed by a deep sigh, and then the voice begins hesitantly. "Like Omar, Wycliffe will be lucky to die a normal death. Not so his followers who will be burned at the stake, disemboweled, drawn and quartered—all in my most civilized of countries. In fact, one follower, Sir John Oldcastle, will be sentenced to be hung and burned alive—both!—a death creatively carried out by suspending him by chains between two gallows over a pyre. For his monstrous audacity to translate the Bible from Latin into the common language of English, Wycliffe himself will not be allowed to rest in peace. The church leaders will order his bones to be disinterred and burnt, and the ashes thrown into a river, which will give rise to the following piece of prophetic poetry:

'*The Avon to the Severn runs,*
The Severn to the sea,
And Wycliffe's dust shall spread abroad,
Wide as the waters be.'"

"Jerome alluded to such atrocities and seemed to condone them. I was hoping it was not true, or, since we are dwelling this night in the future tense of possibility, not certainty—will not be true," says Koheleth disconsolately, looking out the window at the steady light of a planet just coming into view. He takes a deep breath and continues. "Now to my other question about how you came to translate Persian poetry."

"I will develop a passion for languages during my school days at Cambridge University and will translate plays and ballads from Spanish. Knowing my love of Persian, a scholarly friend of mine will show me a rare Oriental manuscript he will stumble upon in the Bodleian Library at Oxford University—Omar Khayyam's poetry. Quite an exquisite little handwritten book, having been produced long before the invention of the printing press."

"Printing press?" interrupts Koheleth.

"A machine that makes multiple copies of a book by means of wood or metal letters that are interchangeable. Covered with ink, they are pressed onto paper. Until its invention, books and scrolls had to be copied one at a time."

"Will my book be printed on a press?"

"Most certainly. In fact, the Bible will be the most printed book in the world."

"Too bad it does not exist already. I need copies made of the final version of my scroll. But please go on."

"This same friend, on taking a professorship in India, will send me a transcription of another manuscript by Omar in the possession of the Bengal Asiatic Society in Calcutta. I will be entranced by the poetry's mix of agnosticism and spare, almost elegiac, Epicureanism, so different from the stultifying Christian piety of my Victorian age. Subversive really. Which is why I will immediately set to work translating the quatrains from Persian. You see, I will be a solitary man as well as a wealthy one, which relieves me of the necessity to earn a living and gives me the privilege of being eccentric. I should explain that in my society only the wealthy can be labeled *eccentric*; a label that allows them to do all sorts of strange things and pursue all sorts of peculiar interests, such as collecting blue butterflies from Siam, pinning them by their rare translucent wings in display cases. Or, in regard to myself, being eccentric enables me to spend my days translating poetry."

"It seems you will lead a pleasant life," remarks Koheleth, "meaning that your prosperity will allow you to do what you want with your mind and time."

"So I will, by and large, apart from failure at marriage—my own fault. Not suited for it, in more ways than one," FitzGerald twitters nervously. "But yes, I will be happy in my private realm of quiet book-lined studies, cottage gardens, and, late in life, boating. I will also be blessed with the close friendship of many poets with whom I will correspond. At its first printing, my little book, published anonymously by Bernard Quaritch, Castle Street, Leicester Square, will receive no attention and will be quickly relegated to the one penny box in front of a bookstore. There it will be spotted by Whitley Stokes who will give copies to the poets Dante Gabriel Rosetti and Algernon Swinburne. They in turn will read it enthusiastically and share it with others, all of them enchanted by its exotic mix of Persian and English. By the end of the century, my version—versions actually, for there will be five—of Omar's *Rabaiyat* will become the most popular book of poetry in the English language. Being not only a poet but even more significantly a great mathematician and astronomer, Omar will have helped to break the connection between science and religion, wreaking, according to the clergy, spiritual havoc."

"Thank you very much," says Omar, obviously pleased with what he takes as a compliment.

"You are welcome. The other man I mentioned, Darwin, will do the same: fissuring the connection, most reluctantly, by showing that all species of life on Earth have evolved from a common ancestor, an idea called natural selection. Man is not at the top of a Great Chain of Being, fixed in form and function from the beginning of time. He is no different from all the other animals—a point you make, Koheleth. Jellyfish, monkey, hyena, earthworm. No matter. All change, not necessarily *improve*, just change, adapting to new circumstances: a broader beak to crack a harder seed; a longer fin to swim in a rougher sea; a bigger brain to out-think a faster predator."

Koheleth yawns, struggling against the desire to shut his eyes. "It sounds as if Darwin will upend the idea of man being formed in the divine image on the sixth day, fixed in time and space, although such a physical description, as prevalent in my generation as in yours, diminishes the immensity of God."

"That Darwin will do. And he will be profoundly troubled, the more so because he will be married to a devout wife whom he loves dearly and does not want to hurt. He will admit in a letter to a friend that he is disturbed by what he calls the 'simple muddle' of his theology, writing, 'I cannot look at the Universe as the result of blind chance, yet I can see no evidence of beneficent Design.'"

"Do you agree?" asks Saadia.

"Let me get my glasses. Where did I put them?" There is a fumbling sound. "My coat pocket? No. Ah, my trousers pocket. Just a minute. I need to clean them off. Smudged. A bit of strawberry jam I think. There, that's

Generations Go, Generations Come

better. And now I will read from the letter I wrote to my friend who first introduced me to Omar's poetry—which is where? Oh, here it is, folded in my vest pocket." He clears his throat and begins to read. "I often think it is not the poetical imagination, but bare science that every day more and more unrolls a greater Epic than the Iliad—the history of the World, the infinites of Space and Time."

Feeling sleepier and sleepier and with the premonition that the following day will require everything he has, Koheleth is still reluctant to ask his visitors to leave. "I have written in my scroll that all creatures have the same breath, and humans have no advantage over animals. Would your troubled Darwin agree?"

"He would," says FitzGerald. "Perhaps your words will provide him with a modicum of comfort. It is a relief to know that the Bible has space for your kind of thinking, that it is more spiritually and intellectually capacious than we narrow Victorians make it. It has the capacity to transcend the work of its translators, a capacity that is true as well of your poems, Omar. For I myself will never be satisfied with my translations. Not at all! I will do the best I can, turning out, as I mentioned, five versions. Your poems will not be the easiest to translate! And there will be so many! I will select what I think is best, giving them a kind of order, as if you began to write your poems at dawn, kept at it through the heat of noonday—under the inverted bowl you call the sky—continued to write as you drank wine with your friends in the cool of the evening, and only put your pen down when you began to fall asleep in a garden with a nightingale singing in the branches. But for all my hard work, I will fall short." There is a kind of plaintive wail from the voice.

"It is the terrible dilemma all translators of poetry face and for which there is no satisfactory solution," says Saadia in a kindly way. "No one wants to sacrifice the music to the meaning or vice versa. I also wrote rubaiyats, both in Hebrew and Arabic, so I know how difficult it is."

"Difficult indeed! I will write to a friend in 1859 that at all cost—let me quote my words precisely," and again there is a rustling, as if of paper, and a clearing of the throat. "A Thing must *live*: with a transfusion of one's own worse Life if one can't retain the Original's better. Better a live sparrow than a stuffed Eagle."

"I use the same phrase but with different animals, specifically a living dog and a dead lion. The lowlier thing that walks under the sun is superior to the majestic thing that lies under the ground. However, it is your use of the word *transfusion* that most impresses me," says Koheleth, "To pour your own lifeblood into the veins of Omar's poems!"

"Some of your translations miss my intent. More like variations on a theme than translations," quips Omar. "In fact, I don't recognize my thoughts. But others! How wonderful your choice of words!" He stops, and then begins to speak slowly, articulating each word:

> *"Ah, make the most of what we yet may spend,*
>
> *Before we too into the Dust descend;*
>
> *Dust into Dust, and under Dust, to Lie,*
>
> *Sans Wine, sans Song, sans Singer, and – sans End!"*

To which Koheleth replies with a yawn, *"Be mindful of your creator in the days of your youth, before the days of trouble come . . . and the dust returns to the earth as it was, and the breath returns to God who gave it. Mist, mist, all is mist."*

And as he says the final phrase, he falls asleep.

9

The Silver Cord is Broken

Koheleth wakes to the silence of his room with a sense of urgency greater than he has ever felt in his life. For the first time in months, the sky is overcast and the air is damp and cool, although no rain has fallen. The scroll is rolled up on the table on the far side of the room. He rises from his bed to walk over to it but is so weak and unbalanced he almost falls. Just in time he grabs his walking stick that he had placed beside his bed the previous evening, close by in case of need. Once it is in his hand, he steadies himself, looking down its sturdy length to where its broad tip meets the wood floor. And that is when he realizes something is wrong, for the stick appears to be much longer than he knows it to be, and his feet seem strangely far away and without feeling, as if disconnected from his legs, which are also strange, being more swollen than normal, accenting the angulation of his withered leg, the one crushed so many years before in the limestone quarry. It is as if his body is a continent that is slowly breaking apart; his toes and feet are already islands; his legs are attenuated peninsulas.

In spite of his unsteadiness, Koheleth wants to review the twelfth chapter of his scroll before the morning's session. Nothing else that he has written is so close to the bone because it is on growing old and dying. The phrase *growing old* confounds him because the verb *to grow* conveys a sense of expansion: the sunflower becoming taller and taller; the melon becoming fatter and sweeter; the child crawling, walking, then running—all growing things reaching ever more toward harvest. Only in the sense of reaching the fullness of the harvest does Koheleth feel the appropriateness of connecting *to grow* with the word *old*, because he does indeed feel full, yet at the same time empty, as if he is a great translucent carapace of a beetle from which the beetle has withdrawn.

Koheleth is not in pain, but there is a pervasive heaviness in his chest and a shallow speed to his breathing, like the panting of a mortally wounded animal. He has felt them several times before, always with an impending sense of doom. Now it is more intense and unrelenting, yet he does not feel that doom. On the contrary, he is peaceful, more curious as to what is about to happen than frightened. Dying is something he has never experienced. He has seen death many times but only as an observer, not as a killer; and, of course, never his own. Will he be able to hear his own death rattles if they occur? Too bad he cannot write down the progression of the symptoms, how one organ after another blinks out like stars disappearing at dawn.

Koheleth's vision is so distorted that as he looks down he perceives of his chest as a sheer cliff from which he is about to plunge. He considers whether he should call his servant or summon Michal, but he decides not to, keeping his mouth shut. He is surprised to discover that he wants to be alone, without the commotion of frowning physicians whose eyes will speak the truth their mouths will not say, as distraught relatives hover around the bed, waiting, waiting.

If his feet appear distant, the scroll is becoming even more distant, looking like a small white chrysalis in the fading light, and with that realization, the urgency he felt on waking evaporates. He gives up the attempt to reach the scroll and lowers himself back down on the bed. There is no reason to make the effort to walk across the room when he knows the words by heart. He begins to murmur them accompanied by the labored sound of his breathing:

> "*Remember your creator in the days of your youth*
> *before the days of trouble come and the years draw near*
> *when you say 'I have no pleasure in them,'*
> *before the sun and the light and the moon and the stars are darkened,*
> *and the clouds return after the rain,*
> *in the day when the guards of the house tremble and the strong men cower,*
> *and the women who grind cease working because they are few,*
> *and those who look through the windows see dimly,*
> *when the doors on the street are shut,*
> *and the sound of the grinding mill is low,*

The Silver Cord is Broken

and one rises up at the sound of a bird,
and all the daughters of song are brought low,
when one is afraid of heights and terror on the way,
the blossoms of the almond tree repulse,
the grasshopper drags itself along, and desire fails."

Koheleth stops and tries to inhale, tensing his chest and neck muscles in the effort. His skin takes on a bluish hue. His hands tingle. When he begins to recite again, it is with great effort; the words come out softer and slower with long pauses in between. Even with the immense difficulty, he appreciates the sound, the separation, the valuing of each syllable as it crosses his tongue:

"Because all go to their eternal home
and the mourners will go through the streets,
before the silver cord is broken
and the pitcher is shattered at the well,
and the wheel is smashed at the cistern
and the dust returns to the earth as it was,
and the breath returns to God who gave it."

Koheleth is drenched in sweat, cold and clammy. He leans forward on the bed to try to catch his breath that is sounding like a thin wheezing with—yes he hears it—a rattle! And with it comes the rush of pain, flooding up to his jaw, down his arm, crushing his ribcage. Suddenly all the air is being sucked out of his lungs, out of the room, out of the sky. In its place, he hears for the first time the patter of rain. It becomes steady and strong, falling on the fig, the date palm, the bald cypress, the redwood, the deodar, the baobab, the eucalyptus, the Arctic willow, the flame tree, the gingko, the bristlecone pine, dripping off their leaves and needles, streaming down their trunks, watering their roots, running into streams that flow to the sea—and the sea is never full.

The End

Scriptural References and Notes

Chapter One

Mist mist all is mist. Eccl 1:2.

Silver life thread, golden bowl. Eccl 12:6.

Ptolemy II Philadelphus, 309–246 BCE, son of Ptolemy I Soter and Berenice. His court was in Alexandria.

"Fools fold their hands." Eccl 4:5–6.

Monsoon is an Arabic word. The winds blow southwest from May to September and then reverse, blowing northeast from November to March. By the third century BCE, trading vessels were crossing the Indian Ocean regularly.

"My vineyard is private." Song of Solomon 8:12. Michal is loosely patterned on the woman in the Song of Solomon, the beloved of the king. She is described as beautiful and independent, refusing to wear a veil, disobeying her brothers, and keeping her own vineyard.

"Two are better than one." Eccl 4:9.

"A cord of three." Eccl 4:12. The line appears in Tablets IV and V in the Epic of Gilgamesh, dating from approximately 2500 BCE, in which Gilgamesh, the king of Sumer, searches for immortality.

Scriptural References and Notes

Targitaos is mentioned by Herodotus, although he is not a translator in Jerusalem.

"The wind blows to the south." Eccl 1:6.

Alexandria was established in 331 BCE by Alexander the Great, although he was there for only a few months. He intended it to be a symbolic link between Greece and Egypt. After his death, his general Ptolemy made the city one of the greatest centers of learning in the world. The library at Alexandria had at its height hundreds of thousands of scrolls. The phrase "the place of the cure of the soul" was inscribed on the wall. The Jewish community in Alexandria was huge, numbering approximately one million by the first century BCE. The city was connected to the Nile by a channel.

Western Sea is the common name for the Mediterranean.

Euclid (c. 325–270 BCE) was a Greek mathematician living in Alexandria during the reign of Ptolemy. His *Elements* is one of the most important works in mathematics, for in it he codified the work of other mathematicians. Euclid proved that the square root of two is irrational and that the number of primes is infinite.

Eudoxus (c. 400–347 BCE) was a Greek mathematician and astronomer whose geometric proofs were incorporated by Euclid.

The phrase uncorrelated possibilities as a definition of chance was used by the British particle physicist and theologian John Polkinghorne.

"There is no royal road." This is one of the few stories that have survived concerning Euclid about whom little is known.

"Of making many scrolls there is no end." Eccl 12:12.

Cahotep's idea of three languages is borrowed from the Rosetta Stone that has on it hieroglyph, Egyptian Demotic, and Greek.

Palm leaves with gold Sanskrit lettering were written with a stylus. The leaves were treated with preservative.

Ega is a language spoken in West Africa.

Scriptural References and Notes

The Pillars of Hercules was the name for the promontories at the opening of the Strait of Gibraltar.

Haudenosaunee refers to the Iroquois and their language. It means people of the long house.

Dzongkha is spoken in Bhutan. It is written in Tibetan script.

As part of the tradition of Sukkot, the mysterious guests are invited into the booth with the words, "Be seated, guests from on high. Be seated, guests of faith, be seated."

"Let your words be few." Eccl 5:2.

Chapter Two

The Hebrew word *debar* means either word or thing.

The Heart Sutra is one of the most famous of the Mahayana Buddhist sutras. There is lack of agreement as to how old it is and whether it was first written in Chinese or Sanskrit.

Bodhisattva Avalokitesvara, meaning "the lord who looks down," is important in Mahayana Buddhism.

Made out of shells, wampum functioned as a proto-language. The Iroquois Confederacy codified in wampum the Haudenosaunee Great Law of Peace. In the tribe's oral tradition there is a warrior turned peacemaker named Ayenwentah (transliterated as Hiawatha) who invented wampum.

"Lord is my shepherd." Ps 23:1.

Fractal. Hausdorff-Besicovitch, named after two mathematicians, is an expression of the dimension of an object, including highly irregular sets.

"What is not there cannot be counted." Eccl 1:15.

"The florets arranged 1,1,2,3,5,8,13,21." This sequence is called the Fibonacci numbers after Leonardo of Pisa, known as Fibonacci, who did not discover it but who made it known in the thirteenth century CE.

Scriptural References and Notes

"Can the crocked be made straight?" Eccl 1:15.

"Of making many scrolls." Eccl 12:12.

Some Hebrew scholars maintain that ezov is mistranslated as hyssop, which is not native to Israel.

"Why is this burning bush." Exod 3:3.

Holy Oil. Exod 30:22–25.

Uvatiarru, pujurak. Inuit and West Greenlandic Inuit.

"You are a god who hides yourself." Ps 88:14.

Chapter Three

"I set my mind." Eccl 8:16–17.

"To recognize the way the heart goes." The phase dates to the third millennium BCE. It is found in the Edwin Smith papyrus (discovered in Luxor in 1862). The phase is: "The counting of anything with the fingers to recognize the way the heart goes."

"For what occurs." Eccl 3:19–21.

Ouroboros. The snake or dragon that eats its tail is found in many cultures including Egypt, Greece and China. The name in Greek means tail devourer.

Hiram's bronze basin and pi. 1 Kgs 7:23; 2 Chr 4.

"He has made everything." Eccl 3:11.

"Again I saw that under the sun." Eccl 9:11.

"Seeking that which has passed away." Eccl 3:15. This passage was important to Dietrich Bonhoeffer while he was in a Nazi prison. In a letter dated December 18, 1943, he wrote: "These last words mean that God gathers up again with us our past, which belongs to us. So when we are seized by

Scriptural References and Notes

a longing for the past – which may happen when we are least expecting it – we can always remind ourselves that that is but one of the many hours which God is holding ready for us." In a following letter, he wrote that the doctrine of the restoration of all things, derived from Ephesians 1:10, was a "magnificent conception, and full of comfort." *Letters and Papers from Prison*. New York: Touchstone Book, Simon & Schuster, 1997, pg. 169.

"For everything there is a season." Eccl 3:1–8.

The blue dye used in the prayer shawl (tallit) came from sea snails and was very valuable. Today blue is used in the flag of Israel.

Chapter Four

Sukkot, the Feast of Booths, occurs in late September and early October.

Zechariah's prophecy. Zech 14:16–19.

"One man among a thousand." Eccl 7:28.

Yo-yo. There exists a fifth century BCE Greek vase that shows a boy playing with a yo-yo.

"I hated my work." Eccl 2:18.

Shepherd from Tekoa. Amos 1:1.

The prophet Jonah ran away from God's command that he go to Nineveh, but in so doing, he was swallowed by a fish.

"What if that poor farmer is a righteous man." Martin Buber relates in *Tales of the Hasidim: Early Masters* the following story: "Once, at the close of the Day of Atonement, when Rabbi Shelomo was in a gay mood, he said he would tell everyone what he had asked of Heaven on these holy days, and what answer was intended for his request. To the first of his disciples who wanted to be told, he said: 'What you ask of God was that he should give you your livelihood at the proper time and without travail, so that you might not be hindered in serving him. And the answer was that what God really wants of you is not study or prayer, but the sighs of your heart, which

Scriptural References and Notes

is breaking because the travail of gaining a livelihood hinders you in the service of God.'" Martin Buber, *Tales of the Hasidim: Early Masters*. New York: Schocken Books, 1970, pg. 280.

The hoopoe bird, common in Israel, dirties its nest with its smelly droppings. The name comes from the sound it makes.

One of the kings of Israel was named Menahem, which means consoler or comforter.

Not all Jews returned to Judah after the exile (586–538 BCE). The Jewish community in Babylon was large.

The oldest extant text of Ecclesiastes is in the Dead Sea scrolls. It was found in Cave 4 at Qumran. Qumran's principal dates of occupation are the first century BCE and the first century CE. However, there is archeological evidence of much older habitation in the area.

"Adding one thing to another." Eccl 7:27.

Ezekiel's wheelworks. Ezek 1:15–16. Several mystical movements grew up around Ezekiel's chariot, known as Merkabah in Hebrew.

"Surely there is not a righteous." Eccl 7:20.

"Never cupped the wind." In Proverbs 30, Agur son of Jakel uses the literary device of listing things in numerical order as a way to compare and contrast.

Chapter Five

"Person who digs a pit." Eccl 10:8–9.

Arimaspoi is the name used by Herodotus who attributed it to Aristeus.

Akkadian cuneiform was used in Mesopotamia from the third through the first millennium BCE.

Gold circlet. A similar armlet with griffins, dating from c. 400 BCE in the Persian Empire, is in the British Museum, London.

Scriptural References and Notes

"Then I saw that all oppressions." Eccl 4:1.

The Turing test was put forward by Alan Turning in 1950 as a way to ask if machines could think, meaning that they could exhibit intelligent behavior typical of a human being.

"Whatever your hand finds to do, do with all your heart." Eccl 9:10.

"If you see a person oppressed in a region." Eccl 5:8.

"Then I saw that all toil. Eccl 4:4.

"For whom am I toiling." Eccl 4:8.

"As you do not know the way of the wind." Eccl 11:5.

Chapter Six

There are many Jewish stories that delve into the idea that all the souls that will ever exist came into being during the seven days of creation. Until their time to take on flesh, they dwell in a treasury or storehouse.

The oldest extant information on the Septuagint is in the pseudonymous *Letter of Aristeas*, which gives an account of how Ptolemy II Philadelphus requested a copy of the Hebrew scripture to be translated into Greek. This story was repeated down through the centuries. Particularly appealing was the claim made by Philo of Alexandria that the seventy translators worked separately only to find that their translations agreed word for word. But nothing is known for certain about the Septuagint except that a translation from Hebrew to Koine Greek was made, probably by several translators over a period of one to two hundred years in Alexandria. The oldest known codices date to the fourth century CE.

Ben Sira is the name of the writer of Ecclesiasticus, also known as Sirach, which is included in the Christian Apocrypha but is not considered canonical by Jews. Ben Sira signs his name in Chapter 50:27 as follows: "Instruction in understanding and knowledge I have written in this book, Joshua (Jesus) son of Eleazar son of Sira of Jerusalem, whose mind poured forth wisdom." The book was translated by his grandson who writes in the

Scriptural References and Notes

Prologue that he himself came to Egypt in the 38th year of the reign of Euergetes. In a remarkable passage, the grandson writes the following: "You are invited therefore to read it [his grandfather's writings] with goodwill and attention, and to be indulgent in cases where, despite our diligent labor in translating, we may seem to have rendered some phrases imperfectly. For what was originally expressed in Hebrew does not have exactly the same sense when translated into another language. Not only this book, but even the Law itself, the Prophecies, and the rest of the books differ not a little when read in the original."

Still spoken in the Indian subcontinent, Tamil dates back at least as early as 300 BCE. Ancient inscriptions in Tamil have been found not only in India and Southeast Asia but also in Egypt.

Rabbi Yohanan ben Zakkai had a school at Jamnia, and it was there that the followers of Hillel gained ascendancy over the followers of Shammai. This had profound implications in the shaping of Rabbinic Judaism. It is not known whether there was actually one council or a series of ongoing discussions.

Shammai and Hillel were important Jewish leaders at the end of the first century BCE and the start of the first century CE. They provided direction for Judaism after the destruction of the temple.

The temple was destroyed in 70 CE by the Roman general Titus. Josephus witnessed the gruesome siege of Jerusalem in which famine claimed many lives. Those who attempted to escape the city were crucified in grotesque positions, up to 500 people a day. Of the final destruction of the temple, Josephus wrote: "While the holy house was on fire, everything was plundered that came to hand, and ten thousand of those that were caught were slain."

"Your holy cities." Isa 64:10–11.

"But the sun and the light and the moon." Eccl 12:2.

Midrash Ecclesiastes is a haggadic commentary on the book.

Jerome was born near Dalmatia and died in Bethlehem. While in Rome, he was close to a circle of wealthy, well-educated woman including Paula and her daughters. His criticism of the clergy was so sharp that after Pope

Scriptural References and Notes

Damasus died, he was forced to leave Rome. His translations were important because they were based on the Hebrew texts and not on the Greek Septuagint. Jerome did not use the word Vulgate.

Didymus was head of the Catechetical School in Alexandria. Jerome spoke of him as Didymus the Seer, but he became known as Didymus the Blind. Ultimately, Jerome opposed the thinking of Origen, distancing himself from Didymus with whom Origen was associated. When Didymus's work became anathema, it was no longer copied by the monks and most of it was lost.

"Provoke her to the contempt of this earthly scene." Jerome, *Preface to the Commentary on Ecclesiastes*, addressed to Paula and Eustochium, Bethlehem, AD 388. Jerome's advice to adopt extreme asceticism may have led to Blesilla's early death. It appears to be one of the reasons for the negativity towards him among the Romans.

The speech by the tavern keeper in the Gilgamesh Epic is as follows: "As for you, Gilgamesh, let your belly be full, enjoy yourself day and night. Find enjoyment every day, dance and play day and night. Let your clothes be clean, let your head be washed, bathe in water. Look upon the little one who holds your hand. Let your wife enjoy herself in your embrace." (Gilg M iii 6–14)

Joyous bridegroom. References to Jesus Christ. John 3:29. Wedding at Cana, John 2:1–11. Cooking breakfast, John 21:9. Prodigal son, Luke 15:11–32.

Chapter Seven

"Eat your bread with gladness." Eccl 9:7.

"Shimmering heat in sunlight." Isa 18:4.

Dietrich Bonhoeffer in his essay *After Ten Years*, written in 1942, wrote of folly and malice as follows: "Folly is a more dangerous enemy to the good than malice. You can protest against malice, you can unmask it or prevent it by force. Malice always contains the seeds of its own destruction, for it always makes men uncomfortable, if nothing worse. There is no defense against folly. Neither protests nor force are of any avail against it, and it is never amenable to reason. If facts contradict personal prejudices, there is

Scriptural References and Notes

no need to believe them, and if they are undeniable, they can simply be pushed aside as exceptions. Thus the fool, as compared with the scoundrel, is invariably self-complacent."

Rig Veda is a collection of Vedic hymns in Sanskrit, dating to the second millennium BCE.

"The wolf shall lie down with the lamb." Isa 11:6.

"The calm words of the wise." Eccl 9:17.

Hezekiah. 2 Chr 32; 2 Kgs 20:20.

"You made a reservoir between the two walls." Isa 22:11.

"In the spirit of knowledge and the awe of the Lord." Isa 11:2–3.

Sira is the name of the writer of Ecclesiasticus. His full name, showing lineage, is Joshua (Jesus) son of Eleazar son of Sira of Jerusalem.

Chapter Eight

Hagar and Ishmael. Gen 16. Gen 25:12–18.

King Belshazzar. Dan 5:5.

"There are righteous people who are treated." Eccl 8:14.

Saadia ben Yosef (892–942 CE) was head (gaon) of the Talmudic academy in Sura. He is important because of his focus on what would eventually be called philology, wherein systematic study was brought to bear on language. To him, revelation in the Torah was critical but to comprehend it required intellectual questioning, scientific in its objectivity. His writings and translations helped open up broad avenues of thought, particularly in Moorish Spain, and then in Europe.

Pharos. Begun approximately 285 BCE, it was one of the Seven Wonders of the World. It was badly damaged by earthquakes and by 1480 CE was destroyed.

Scriptural References and Notes

Omar Khayyam (1046–1122 CE) was born in Nayshapur. He was revered as a mathematician, astronomer, philosopher and poet. His *Treatise on Demonstration of Problems of Algebra* was transmitted to Europe where it was highly influential. He also wrote *Explanation of the Difficulties in the Postulates of Euclid*. It is reported that he demonstrated to a prestigious audience that Earth is not the center of the universe. But he is best known for his rubáiyát, meaning quatrains, of which there may have been more than a thousand.

"The sun rises and the sun sets." Eccl 1:5.

"The Lord has set a tent in the heavens." Ps 19:4–5.

Heracleides. Greek astronomer, fourth century BCE, who suggested the rotation of Earth.

For information on Edward FitzGerald, see the biography written by Robert Bernard Martin, *With Friends Possessed: A Life of Edward FitzGerald*. New York: Atheneum, 1985. All quotes from FitzGerald are found in that book.

John Wycliffe (1320–1384) was an English theologian who disagreed with the Roman Catholic Church on a number of issues. Working with his assistants, including Nicholas of Hereford, he completed the translation from the Vulgate into English in 1382. His followers, the Lollards, were persecuted without mercy.

Edward Cowell introduced FitzGerald to the works of Omar Khayyam.

Great Chain of Being is a classical concept of the world's hierarchical structure.

In 1870, Darwin wrote to his friend Joseph Hooker, "I cannot look at the Universe as the result of blind chance, yet I can see no evidence of beneficent Design."

"Be mindful of your creator in the days of your youth." Eccl 12:1.

SCRIPTURAL REFERENCES AND NOTES

Chapter 9

Eccl 12.

Sukkot marks the end of the yearlong reading of the Pentateuch and the beginning again with Genesis. The joyful day following the seventh day of Sukkot is called Simhat Torah. Deuteronomy, the last book in the Pentateuch, closes with the death of Moses.

www.ingramcontent.com/pod-product-compliance
Lightning Source LLC
Chambersburg PA
CBHW050831160426
43192CB00010B/1987